*radiant living*

renewal of health and well being

since 1977

Unity Church
414 - 31st Street
Des Moines, IA 50312

radiant living

the challenge of change

JUANITA ORTON KEITH

Introduction: **JAMES AUTRY**

Archer Creative Press
P.O. Box 7087
Grand Station
Des Moines, Iowa
50309

Copyright © 1990 by Juanita Orton Keith

All rights reserved
including the right of reproduction,
except for short excerpts used as
support material, with credit
to this book.

Library of Congress
Catalog Card No.: 90-85331
Publisher's ISBN: 0-9628351-0-2

Also by Juanita Orton Keith

**YOUR RADIANT BODY,
A PICTURE OF HEALTH**
foreword by Dr. Elmer Green
of the Menninger Foundation,
Topeka, Kansas

First Printing, October 1980
Second Printing, May 1981

DEDICATED

*To all who seek
to come home to
Radiant Living.*

**Acknowledgement, with gratitude for support,
in the publication of this book:**

Janet Krieg, early reading of manuscript
and thoughtful feedback

Marilyn Nussbaum, artful calligraphy

Jerry Miller, professional wisdom

Greg Morrill, creative artwork

Vicki Spurgin, for her sensitivity in
shaping the bodycopy

Don Keith, my husband since June 1942,
solid and supportive

All who have participated in Radiant Living Workshops,
and inspired the creation of this book.

CONTENTS

INTRODUCTION BY JAMES AUTRY

CHAPTER I   COME HOME TO RADIANT LIVING 1
    The Components of Radiant Living: Change, Infinite Wisdom and Infinite Love
    Visualization in Radiant Living
    Barriers to Radiant Living
    Radiant Living Formula: 1) Sort Out, 2) Choose Priorities, 3) Allow Endings, and
        4) Look at Alternatives
    Radiant Living Brings Change
    Experience of Change in Nature
    Radiant Living, a New Cycle Beginning with the first Radiant Body Workshop
    Endings and Beginnings
    The Birthing Rite as Change
    Leaving Sophistication for the Simple Life
    A Significant Dream
    In Summary

CHAPTER II   WORRY, A BARRIER TO RADIANT LIVING 17
    The Tide of Love
    Energy, the Basis for Trust
    Trust Begins With You
    Allow the Seeds of Trust to Blossom
    Trust Verified Scientifically
    A List of Worry One-Liners
    In Summary

**CHAPTER III   ANGER AND FEAR, BARRIERS TO
RADIANT LIVING** 27
    The Power of Memory in Demonstration
    Pitirim A. Sorokin, An Apostle of Love
    Radiant Living Workshops
    An Experience of Infinite Wisdom and Infinite Love
    Anger In Its Many Faces
    Anger Is Energy
    The Dynamics of Anger
    Techniques for Dealing With Anger
    Fear In Its Many Faces
    In Summary

CHAPTER IV   JEALOUSY, WHAT DOES IT MEAN? 45
    Start By Owning Your Jealousy
    Wisdom and Love Suggest a New Approach to Jealousy
    In Summary

CHAPTER V   ORDER IN THE UNIVERSE 49
    Desire and Discipline in the Discovery of Order
    Clutter Creates Chaos
    Garden Weeds as Clutter
    Allow the Order of the Universe Into Your Life
    In Summary

CHAPTER VI   FINITE MIND EXPERIENCES INFINITE WISDOM 59
    Infinite Wisdom is for All
    Normal Experiences Often Seem Like Miracles
    Another Experience with Infinite Wisdom
    In Summary

CHAPTER VII   HEALING, AN ADVENTURE IN RADIANT LIVING 69
    Cells as the Unit of Energy
    Energy, the Agent in Self-Healing
    Experiencing the Cell
    Attract and Radiate
    Experience Your Own Healing
    My Experience of Healing
    In Summary

CHAPTER VIII   DIET AND NUTRITION IN SELF-HEALING 85
    Three Basic Food Nutrients
    Four Basic Food Categories
    Food Quality in Proportionate Quantity
    Corporate America Endorsing Nutrition
    In Summary

CHAPTER IX   EXERCISE IN SELF-HEALING 91
    Hypokinetic Disease
    What Is Muscle?
    The Treatment of Clutching Muscles
    The Character of Fitness
    Benefits of Moderate Exercise
    A Reminder on Smoking
    In Summary

**CHAPTER X   RADIANT LIVING ADAPTS TO DISEASE OR
DISABILITY THAT WILL NOT LET GO** 103
    Healing Energy As Power
    Pain-Relief Through Endorphins and Enkephalins
    What Is Pain?
    Chinese Qi Gong, Acupuncture and Moxibustion In Experience
    Beijing Institute of Technology
    Syntropy as Negative (Reverse of) Entropy, Relative to Qi Gong
    Three Essentials in Practice of Qi Gong
    Specific Cures Through Qi Gong
    The Life Energy of Qi As Life Information
    Pertinent Facts on Acupuncture As Healing and Adaptive Measures
    In Summary

EPILOGUE: ANTICIPATING THE GLOBAL FAMILY 125

INTRODUCTION

I first met Juanita O. Keith about 25 years ago. She signed up as a student in a free-lance writing class I was teaching as part of the adult education program in the Des Moines city schools.

Little did I know that, 25 years later, I would be writing an introduction to her *second* book. If I could claim credit for "teaching" Juanita how to write, I would, but I know that her writing comes from deep within herself. It is the natural outgrowth of her own experience in growing and learning and seeking what Don Juan called the "path with heart."

Juanita is still growing and learning, and fortunately for the rest of us, she is also teaching. In this, her second book, she brings her special insights into a way of being which she herself works to personify, Radiant Living.

In so doing, Juanita cuts through some of the fluffy stuff that so often surrounds these subjects, and gives us definitions and examples and clear guidelines for achieving the radiance.

She draws from her own experience, both in the living of her life and in her private practice working with others, to share her vision of a life in which we continue, as she has, to grow and learn, and yes, to teach others.

I am very happy that my path has once again crossed the path of Juanita Orton Keith. Only this time, it's her turn to teach me.

                                              James A. Autry
                                              Des Moines, Iowa

---

James Autry is much in demand nationally for poetry readings from his three published collections: *Nights Under a Tin Roof; Life After Mississippi,* and *Love and Profit, The Art of Caring Leadership.* In 1989 Autry appeared on the Public Broadcasting System (PBS) as a featured poet. The program was Bill Moyer's television 6-part series, The Power of the Word.

CHAPTER ONE

Come Home to Radiant Living

You are invited to Radiant Living. Come as you are. There is no judge, no jury, no threatening influence. Sit in silence and listen as one who seeks the truth.

Radiant Living is a way to all there is; it is the truth.

Understand, there are many credible paths, and you may choose as it best serves you according to your lifetime orientation. But know that the truth is the truth is the truth, no matter how it is presented.

Radiant Living is the truth; it is a way to all there is.

Radiant Living is grounded in the energy of your body. You are a system of electrochemical and electromagnetic processes. Through these processes, your body is activated and anchored as your contemporary home on earth. These processes complete all the unique chores of renewing trillions of cells so that your body reacts to its own stimulus. These same processes keep every cell correctly communicating with other cells, like the social structure of interrelationships person to person.

In Radiant Living you are extraordinary. You discover that your Spirit is secure, anchored by a magnificent Radiant Body. This is the truth. "An ego trip?" you ask. No, not at all! Believe, for if you reject the truth, your body withers and becomes prone to illness. When you accept the truth, you radiate; your body flourishes. You stand tall. You fulfill your potential. And you are so busy doing, you don't have time to pretend through ego games.

In total, your energy is creative: During mitosis, or the splitting of cells, photon radiation sends out waves of light. If you doubt this, perhaps you say, "I can't see any light." This is the purest; it is ultraviolet, beyond what is visible to the human eye as yet. Further, in Radiant Living you don't have to see to believe.

Listen again to the marvel of your creative energy: During mitosis your cells also emit sound, ultrasonic sound beyond what your ears can hear.

In Radiant Living, you light up this world; you sound forth with joy.

You are invited to Radiant Living. Come as you are. Be at home in the silence which greets you. Learn to know the beauty of Radiant Living and become that beauty.

The Components of Radiant Living

There are three components to remember in Radiant Living: Change, Infinite Wisdom and Infinite Love.

Change is everywhere in life. It is in the seasons of nature. We look to nature as the model for we are one with nature. Change seems mundane, but it is highly relevant to the enactment of Radiant Living. If you decide to embrace Radiant Living, expect change in who you are and ultimately in your outer circumstances. You will change as the "seasons" of your mind initiate change.

Infinite Wisdom and Infinite Love are the nurturing components of Radiant Living. You'll see that you need them both. Wisdom tells you how to apply Love as compassion in its nurturing concern. Without the Wisdom to interpret, Love may go astray and be misused. As the first step, accept the healing of Love for yourself, so that you develop the power to do your part in healing the world. Infinite Wisdom and Infinite Love are in constant supply from the Spirit Source, always available. Learn to accept what you need. Nobody *gives* you Wisdom and Love, so don't beg. Simply affirm that you already have all that you need. As often as you feel inadequate, claim more. Claim it in silence with Spirit guidance. If you are Christ oriented, seek your answers from Jesus. Otherwise, follow your own inner guidance from the Source as you know it.

Visualization in Radiant Living

As an aid in demonstrating Radiant Living, you may want to use visualization to penetrate the subconscious. If you like, in this regard, think of Radiant Living as a colorful, sturdy umbrella. Picture it being woven from threads of your own peaceful energy vibrations, evoked by your thoughts and emotions. So that in effect, you weave the substance of your umbrella, and then in the use of visualization you engineer its construction. When fully shaped, it becomes an invisible shield.

The handle of your umbrella is the shape of your determination to build and *hold onto* all that is high purpose in your interpretation of Radiant Living. In essence, your umbrella in easy access — you can unfold it at will from your pocket — becomes your shield from life's turbulence. This is psychologically sound because outer turbulence must always be countered by inner peace and that is the substance you used in constructing your umbrella shield.

Barriers to Radiant Living

Radiant Living is a commitment to joy and trust, replacing worry, anger and fear, jealousy, and all the related barriers that ultimately bring you pain and distract you from clarity of mind. These barriers are akin to stress and anxiety. They are not resolved in the wink of an eye or the wave of a hand. Barriers entrench themselves over a period of time, and it usually takes even a longer period of time to eliminate their hold. Begin by being alert to what is happening in your life. Know that worry, anger and fear, and jealousy have long and tenacious roots. Don't just whack away; dig down to the source of the barrier.

Whenever you feel uncomfortable, mentally or physically, know that is your alert to question what is happening. If you believe in Radiant Living, you will shift into internal silence and ask. Even when you are busily engrossed in the outer world, you can train yourself to shift into inner awareness, momentarily. In time, you will get instant feedback to avert an impending collision course.

Whatever your current pain, others can match it from their lifetime of intermittent agonies. This is to say to you that you never need feel isolated by your pain. As you read some of the episodes of life written into this book, you will identify from your own pain. A note to remember is that you can let go of pain whenever you are ready. However, no one is judging your perception of pain. No one is badgering you to let go; no one is commanding you to do it, now. You are in charge, making decisions, mentally laying out your strategy from practices in Radiant Living. The mental process always precedes the experience. Remember, as long as you claim your uncomfortable circumstances by making excuses, you will remain locked into them. Change your mindset to change your life.

What happens as you read this, is that your conscious mind is asking, "Shall we give it a try? Shall we risk Radiant Living? I hear it demanding change...what are the risks?"

Meanwhile, the subconscious mind is quite neutral. It says, "Tell me what we want; I'm listening without judgment; I'm ready to process whatever you tell me." And then it whispers something about not bombarding it with a blizzard of confusing answers, like "Yes, I want change, but no, I don't want the risk of change." Such answers yank and pull one way and then the other. The subconscious cannot do other than follow the conscious mind's directives. So be consistent in what you wish to achieve. Even in the midst of pain and turmoil, affirm your continued goal.

Radiant Living Formula

The formula for easing into Radiant Living is simply stated, but only discipline can enact it. Discipline is your responsibility. In Radiant Living no one disciplines another. Radiant Living as a protective umbrella allows no complacency. You need to remain alert to your motives and your direction. Within this pattern is a way of life in which you cooperate and direct, in which you enact, and which works for you at your bidding:

Here is the structure of that formula: 1) sort out, 2) choose priorities, 3) allow endings, and 4) choose alternatives that alert you to develop the design for your new age of thinking. That thinking will lead you onto your path.

To clarify the formula, we will look at each step individually:

1) **Sort Out** — Choose a time when you can start with meditation, at the least a ten-minute period of silence. Have pencil and paper handy and within or after the meditative silence, list all the current activities you have on your schedule. Think about this carefully, and list everything that takes your time, including your bed rest and sleep. List all of this without any attempt to judge. When you have a complete list, ask yourself, "Am I doing too much? Do I feel harried, frustrated, tired?" Be honest with yourself. If the answer is "Yes," that leads to the second step:

2) **Choose Priorities** — Starting with the number one, evaluate the most important item in your above listing. Continue to number, down to the very last item on your list. If some are equally important, group them together. The effectiveness of this formula depends upon honest assessment.

To begin with, in this whole process you have acknowledged that your inner peace is being skewed, or misaligned, by trying to do too much. In other words, your energy doesn't cover all you presently *think* you must do. So the activities with the latest numberings have to go. That is your decision.

3) **Allow Endings** — Putting closure on an activity is nearly always painful. Whether you can endure that pain depends upon how determined you are to "come home to Radiant Living." The bonus feature to remember is that you will be more effective in what you choose to continue.

An example from my life, years ago, was letting go of the delightful craft work I did, such as sewing and crocheting. At a time when I was determining to develop my writing, the crafts, I realized, were usurping my time and my energy. I fully enjoyed making my own wardrobe, and creating sweaters or afghans for every new arrival in my family or friends' families. But something had to go, and that, reluctantly, was my decision.

Check yourself out in making endings. Are you playing ego games? That was what my sewing was, I decided. I could be better dressed for the same money if I did my own sewing and styling. But it became less important to me, finally, than establishing my potential as a writer.

In summary, endings are crucial. Without endings, we never get on to the next step. My next step was to develop a writing career so that I could promote the joys and discipline of Radiant Living.

4) **Alternatives that Alert You** to develop the design for your true purpose in this lifetime. To work this out, allow yourself the time to get into the silence of your inner person, so that you come into the flow of Wisdom and Love. An important discipline of Radiant Living is utilizing Infinite Wisdom and Infinite Love through Spirit alignment. When you do, serendipity will rearrange your life, putting you into the right place at the right time. Establishing the flow, is what we call it in Radiant Living. When it begins to happen, don't bother to climb the flagpole and shout about the changes to all the world. They don't care. Just smile and bask in your new role as everything *slowly* comes together for you. *Slowly* is the word. Serendipity seldom smashes and crashes its way. It works quietly and effectively. Then one day you will feel it as a mighty surge, and that will herald your own new age awakening.

Radiant Living Brings Change

You may not yet be ready to undergo the rigors of Radiant Living discipline. It would be well to read this entire book and get a feeling for the full picture. Get a feel for the peace of mind that grows with Radiant Living. It was, indeed, that peace of mind that sparked my decision to share with a wider audience than those few in the earlier Radiant Living Workshops. My goal is to serve as a catalyst to those who come as they are, in search of a wider truth than they have thus far understood, with a goal of practicing more of their potential.

In Radiant Living there is constant change. Without change, life becomes stagnant. One moment you may be saying, "My life is just what I want," yet wake up in the next moment to a drastic need for change, unanticipated change.

Experience of Change In Nature

We may explore the roots of change by going back to the pattern of nature. I have lived all these years in the upper midwest where nature changes regularly, four seasons of the year. In that setting, sometimes nature's change seems abrupt, or is it simply abrupt to my awareness? In early spring the trees seem to be sleeping one day, and suddenly there are nodules that with the first warm day burst into green "lace" which with continued warmth rapidly become leaves of full pattern.

Fall is another good example. It is, at least in the Fall, my favorite season. It is a time when I especially indulge in poignant recollections of change in nature's way. Those recollections take me on a "trip" in which I relive the nostalgia of Fall and what it meant to me in rural mid-America years ago, on the farm of my childhood near St. Cloud, Minnesota. I've relived that "trip" so often. It begins as regularly as nature cools from the hot and humid summers in Iowa where I have been at home since the early '50s. During those earlier days in St. Cloud, I climbed our hill topped with ageless trees and constantly burgeoning underbrush to revel in a blaze of changing colors. That vivid setting was like a crown of glory to our family farm. It was my world. I tramped there at will, radiant with joy, down my favorite path that wound through a child's paradise. It was a blessing of bird calls, scurrying small animals and the smells of nature.

Austere farm life offered me that special bonus of change during each of four seasons; but as I reminisce now, I remember Fall best of all.

Presently it is late October here in Iowa. These are city streets, yet nature is everywhere and everything to me, a model of change. Walking briskly in dawning sunlight, I am aware that the trees, long time friends in my daily walks, are dressed now in nostalgic hues of red and gold and brown, like the trees on my hill at home on the farm. It is as if this present scene is focused within the old-time family treasure, a 3-D hand-held viewer that brought the image right before the eye. And in my present exhilaration, every detail of nature becomes exquisite. Certainly this Fall change has been in process for some time, but this early morning I am intensely aware of it. These feelings are toneless echoes from the Fall season and that Minnesota farm hill so vivid in memory. It is the ecstacy of autumn's symphony accompanying seasonal voices in full chorus: a rhapsody and a dance of all that is important to me at this moment.

I remember that every Fall is a poignant ending, yet every seasonal ending initiates the spell of new beginnings. In panoramic flashback I visualize trees coming into the green of Spring's magnificent foliage. I see those trees weathering the sun's heat, the clouds' rain, and the welcome cool of nights as the Summer pattern is altered again and again. Those same trees of Spring's green, now wear autumn's hues and will slowly shed that costume, soon to be left naked in seasonal lethargy when it is Winter's turn.

Endings. No more summer heat and humidity. Before long there will be arctic winds whipping through barren branches, a howling new song, different key, another full chorus. On occasion, ice will be the indomitable guest. Its load will come bowing and breaking branches, seemingly lifeless to the plunder. Full Winter heralds an ending to vibrant tree life as whirling snow cements its grasp to rough tree bark. Even so, tree life remains on hold, remembering it has a Spring date to rebirth and reclaim its green dress of beauty. And so the cycle continues.

Throughout life, change is constant not only in nature. Change is a challenge. Sometimes that change is devastating, but that feeling, too, shall pass and what emerges are lessons well learned. Memory serves best when it recalls both the joys of pleasure and the lessons from pain. If all the seasonal Fall meant were the death of the leaves, it could not possibly spark such joy in nature, such oneness with rapture as it does for so many Fall addicts. The succession of Falls I've witnessed in all of its past and present unique splendor, reminds me, reassuringly, that life is a series of cycles; and I am free to choose the reaction that fits my mood in any given time frame. Let it most often be heightened joy, yet I know that joy is often laced with pain.

Radiant Living, A New Cycle

Radiant Living has been for me a phase of life as definite as childhood. It is a cycle that began with my own new age of understanding. Officially, Radiant Living began in July 1977 with the first Radiant Body Workshop. Twelve people participated, six men and six women. In between childhood, which climaxed when I moved from my farm home at age eighteen, and the Radiant Body Workshops were many years of exciting, sometimes tedious and heart-rending preparations for this current phase. Difficult lessons had to be learned in experiencing a vast range of emotional changes. Learning difficult lessons is a universal growth pattern for everyone.

In reality, this cycle of Radiant Living may have begun when I was born. Did that infant mind in the following years enjoy the right to be mothered? Did it traumatize briefly over the first separation from true mothering when a wayward character plucked me from my car basket during the first summer of my life? So they tell me, I had awakened from a nap in the back seat of our open, touring car parked on the county fair grounds. My family had wandered off to take in the show of fruits, vegetables, animals, and farm machinery of that day. No one thought about child abduction in those years, in that country setting. Luckily for all concerned, a grounds attendant at that Benton County Fairgrounds had watched the seeming abduction, sensing there was something awry when a strolling, lone woman happened onto a crying baby, unattended in a parked car. He watched her disappear into the bleachers, baby in arms, and reported the scene when my family returned to the empty car. No problem, I was quickly recovered.

At a later time, when I was just fourteen months old, how was this person I grew to become, affected by the sudden death of my mother during the World War I flu epidemic? Perhaps that trauma of separation and change helped me as well as my two sisters and two brothers to be survivors — no matter what life's lessons.

Our father a year later married our mother's younger sister who had a vastly different personality from our mother's quiet ways. The fiery, temperamental nature brought great change into our home, from that younger sister.

That new union added to our family, first a half-sister who died during birth, and then a half-sister who was inordinately protected by her mother throughout her childhood. She was so protected that to a degree it led to subconscious rejection of her by the rest of us who often felt emotionally neglected.

That may well have been no one's fault, but simply a factor in the pattern of drastic change: a man — our father — trying to cope with the loss of a wife, who was also his companion, and mother of his first five children. And in his loss, over-compensating for the needs of his second wife, Daisy, a woman who had lost a sister to whom she was very close, yet who felt repeatedly rejected by her sister's children. They were doing no more than bewilderingly protesting that she might attempt to fill their beloved mother's shoes. She had been Aunt Daisy to all of us. Now, suddenly, she was Mama Daisy, too drastic a change particularly for my older brother who, I recall, addressed her as Aunt Daisy all through the years.

All of us were too young to appreciate that Mama Daisy in marrying Dad was helping him to keep us all together under one roof. Nevertheless, that marriage brought many changes, some of them difficult, but on the positive side surely we have all learned to be survivors even when circumstances create temporary trauma.

Endings and Beginnings

Endings and beginnings are a process of life which demonstrates as change. Change is inherent. Change is growth. Change is everywhere, in the physical body, in the mind, and in the universe.

Change is a partner with *trust*. The two work most effectively when cooperating with the partners of finite mind and the Infinite Mind of God. Some call it the Infinite Mind of the Universe, or the Mind of All that is. Whatever your orientation, it is effective to affirm, "I *trust* God's Plan for my life." Such a trust allows change to heal and rectify individual life. I don't begin to fully understand that process of change, but whether or not I understand it, I know it to be truth. I *trust*.

Perhaps a deep-seated awareness of trust began from a lesson thrust upon me when I was fourteen months old, through the death of my mother. Where had that significant person gone? I could not find her. She simply disappeared. I was too young to understand what had happened to her. She wasn't in bed, she wasn't in the kitchen, she wasn't outside or in the barn. She was gone. But life went on. There must be many different ways that trust begins for a toddler. For me, trust inadvertently grew out of the aftermath of losing my mother.

At this point in life I can see that trust has been a force in shaping my life. Trust in change has built many bridges to carry me from one phase into another. Trust in the ultimate makes life so easy: Life begins to flow without the rigors of trying to stake it out in logical terms through the mind that analyzes and agonizes.

Change in the finite realm is saying goodbye and closing the door. Trust is knowing that tomorrow another door will open into new experience. The best of change is the freedom to move without regret, or with minimal pain, from one space to another. Trust is knowing that endings anticipate a turning point. I have found life to be a pattern of exciting change experienced whenever I am willing to let go of the past and look to the future without excessive fear. Indeed, fear is eased as I perceive that there is no future; only the now, a day at a time.

The Birthing Rite as Change

The initiation to change comes universally in moving from fetus to infant. After considerable research, psychologists are now telling us the birthing process may indeed be relevant to how we accept future change. The warm, comfortable protection of the mother's body nurturing the fetus would seem to be a state that rebuffs change. In fact, is that the reason some births are more difficult than others? The fetus resists change, some more than others. Yet when the gestation time is ripe for delivery, ripe for change, nature's excitement and precision at the birthing process is unsurpassed. It is the turning point which according to many indicates the beginning of life. The transition from fetus to infant is crucial. The birthing rite, including the medical development of the C-Section, is the only way from the womb to the free-world. It brings us slowly, or abruptly in some cases, into the world where we become a life functioning on its own. We blossom into a physical body of electro-chemical processes which develops and manifests according to our own thoughts and emotions, a body in constant change through cycles of growth. We begin a life of joy and pain, a life shaped by choices. And if we could but remember it, that phenomenal birthing rite should remind us that we are a part of the great orderly Plan of Life. We do not live in isolation.

Although the birthing rite is a personal experience of separation for mother and fetus, being born is a universal experience common to all of us. If we live, we have been born. We are born to live in this lifetime until that point of separation commonly called death.

If we could retain the simplicity of that infant state into which we are spawned, if our culture could recognize and reverse the hyprocrisy of sophistication, joy could sustain us for a lifetime. Pain develops only as we create barriers. Barriers such as worry and fear and anger interfere with the harmonious flow of life which is our heritage, a heritage of health and wholeness. It is a heritage of perfection in as much as we are aware that we are One with God, one with Universality of Life.

Leaving Sophistication For The Simple Life

Radiant Living is one of today's patterns which deals with the pain of barriers we create for ourselves, barriers which repel change. After many years of the subterfuge of pseudo-sophistication, it is not easy to find one's way back to the simple and abundant life. Yet in Radiant Living there are techniques which help to shape attitudes. The pattern is a lifestyle of joy, developing from the stimulation of confronting and surmounting one's own personality barriers. These barriers can be as varied and unique as any given personality.

Radiant Living's characteristic joy thrives on change, builds on each comfortable success. To repeat, this exciting pattern includes the process of 1) sorting out, 2) choosing priorities, 3) allowing endings and 4) studying the alternatives to fresh beginnings. Flexibility is the mode of Radiant Living, a flexibility that invites change wherever it prospers one's life into wholeness. It speaks to being able to adapt at that time when it is in one's best interest to adapt, and to have the courage to take the risk.

Prolonged rigidity is often folly, yet it seemingly allows for more security at any present moment. Adapting to one's own need may even mean moving out of one's present space into an entirely new one. And how personally threatening that change may be. Or how stimulating!

At times we just naturally flow with change. That is healthy. Then again the fear of the unknown, or anger over one's environment stalls or diverts that change. Nevertheless, change at the right time is crucial to health and wholeness. And aborted change which creates disappointment and stymies growth will ultimately manifest as body illness. I have found it to be so in experience. Check it out in your own life.

When we allow change to flow we create a setting for innate talent. Such a setting encourages creativity and intuition as partners to the analytical and logical mind. Research shows that innate talent blossoms through the harmonious functioning of the right-brain and the left-brain hemispheres in a mental partnership. The flow of change is both physiological and psychological.

For you or me individually the Radiant Living pattern creates inner balance, building into external radiance. In healing ourselves we become participants in healing our world. There is a great deal of help available to us, for we have today an unseen Hierarchy making significant input for change through our human energy, a change for Good throughout the universe. Such change is facilitated by individuals in many groups and Radiant Living is but one of them. For years Radiant Living was strictly Iowa based, but eventually it began to ripple out nation-wide through national sales of the book, YOUR RADIANT BODY, and the tape, JOY, RELAXATION AND HEALING. Internationally, the book and sometimes the tape as well, may be found in India, the Soviet Union, China and countries of Europe.

You are invited to participate in Radiant Living, to form your own support group for studying and practicing the concepts of the above book. This book on change is a companion to YOUR RADIANT BODY. Belonging to Radiant Living does not mean paying dues or membership fees within a structure. Rather, it means the will to make responsible choices for health and wholeness within the dynamic process of change, to whatever extent you are ready to experience that change.

A Significant Dream

Before the Radiant Living Program had its name, when it was in the process of developing as a thought form, I had a significant dream. It is recorded in detail in my Dream Journal, but following is the capsule thought that came through my personal dream process: I had struggled up a sheer granite wall. It was not the wall of a simple garden enclosure, but of mountainous proportions. I believe the granite quarries in St. Cloud, Minnesota (where I was born) are significant to that, in that I was climbing out of my birthplace, moving on. The climb was not the thing that stood out in my dream; it was, rather, the barren plateau stretching out before me after I had made the climb. Change is what it meant. The top of the granite wall was the symbol of an ending of a difficult journey, a turning point. There was clearly no going back, and what lay ahead was truly a challenge. There are no finite words to describe the full impact of that dream in my own awareness at the time of the dream. It was a new space, my own space.

That dream has universal significance. When we master one difficult climb, more specifically when a particular phase of life comes to an end, we stand ripe for the change which heralds another beginning. At first, we may not have any idea what that change will be, but the important thing is to let go, to detach from what has ended.

It is so crucial to let go of the old for that allows the energy necessary to launch into the new. It could be a loss of a job. It could be the loss of a spouse in death or divorce. It could be a major change in living — a new lifestyle or location. It could even be an awakening of how to better understand and adapt while staying with a difficult marriage or job relationship. In such cases, it would mean letting go of the old pain so that joy could develop between the same two more flexible and understanding partners as they prepare for a future together, living one day at a time in harmony.

In my own life at the time of the dream, I had recently completed four years of college at fifty-eight years of age. Typical of a student at any age, my question for some time had been, "What next?" Working with people as a catalyst in their search for health and wholeness was the goal that had sent me back to college at fifty-four. But precisely how was that goal to develop? Again and again I reprogrammed that dream, searching for the answer. What was to develop on that barren plateau stretching out before me at the top of that granite mountain climb? No matter how many times I brought that dream back, the plateau remained barren.

Dreams take time to develop into a logical interpretation. And developing ideas only come as we are ready to receive them. My impatience was a barrier for some time. Eventually, from dreams and waking meditation I gathered three phrases to guide me: I would "birth my own baby," there would be "no footprints to follow," and I could not "cling to another's coattails." This seemed to indicate that I should not expect to move into an established program, but, rather, that I must start a new project. Gradually the concepts for the Radiant Body Workshops began to flow through from Infinite Wisdom and Infinite Love. At times I was deeply motivated and it all seemed so simple. Then again the mandate that "You are in charge," was frightening. Trust, or the lack of it, was my problem. The barren plateau stared back at me. I had to sit on that barren plateau for a long time before it came to me that the very Power which helped me to climb that granite mountain would also help me to do whatever I was supposed to do. I just had to stand up squarely on my own two feet and accept that Power.

The Power which is God, or Universal Energy, or Positive Thoughts — whatever we may choose to call it — is potent. It is the Power which is motivating the New Group of World Servers, referred to by the people of the Lucis Foundation in New York City, who are affiliated with the Alice Bailey books.

In Summary

For the most part, I choose to dwell on the constructive changes in my life, yet remembering that all change is significant. Change has shaped my life, and is filling in the plateau I climbed so diligently during my dream state in 1976.

Within the pattern of change I find challenge as I am drawn over and over again to 1) sort out, 2) choose priorities, 3) allow endings, and 4) study alternatives that would alert me to develop the new design meant to emerge.

One of the prerequisites to change, is to recognize that change is due — or even overdue. Sometimes when change is the most imminent, I am the least alert to it. It is like not being able to see the forest for the trees. Then in retrospect, after the change is in swing, I look back and see that I had turned into the course even before I knew it. Has it happened that way for you?

CHAPTER TWO

Worry, A Barrier To Radiant Living

Worry is a potential power which threatens Radiant Living. In extreme worry, that power multiplies into a kind of rampage. Yet worry's potential is useless unless we empower it by allowing worry to take over our lives.

Trust is the antidote. *Trust* is the silencer to that rampage of worry. Take the power invested in worry and reinvest it in *trust*.

How do you make this reinvestment? Start by utilizing the affirmation, "I *trust* God's (the Universal) plan for my life; I *trust* beyond all limitations." When a rampage of worry threatens your peace of mind, hold steady to your affirmation. Never waver. Affirm repeatedly, every time your concern comes to mind.

There have been periods in my life when I knew from lessons learned that the only alternative to holding steady was to be inundated by the perils of worry. It was a test of Radiant Living to hold steady. Through *trust*, definite dividends always appeared. It helped the process to consciously accept them and to remember to give thanks. So I continue to *trust, to trust beyond all limitations.* At the darkest hour, that is my alert to *trust* all the more.

On the surface, there is logical cause to worry. The entire world appears to be a legitimate stage for it. Physical violence is rampant. In the printed and electronic media the widest newscoverage is given to pockets of war and lethal crime. It is as if violence were inadvertently being abetted by a public relations campaign to keep it flourishing. As a result, the collective subconscious has become inundated with worry, giving it power worldwide. And that which is all around us in society, zaps our personal lives as well. The pattern of worry is fully pervasive.

Yet there are millions today courageously looking beyond the blatant carnage of physical violence and profound mental upsets. They are the ones who care enough about the survival of this civilization to plan for and enter into the change for Good. What some have termed the dark hours, are more accurately the very stimulus promoting a new age of individual and ultimate global change.

The Tide of Love

A great tide of Love is the foundation for that change. Humanity is ingenious in survival tactics, and creative thinking has never been more welcome, more refreshing, more crucial. This incoming tide of Love is powerful; it is like an insurrection to abolish the violence which at times seems to be in control, worldwide. Through *trust*, the power of Love is emerging and Love is so all encompassing that worry pales in its glow. Life is basically good and violence is simply a by-product of a confused mindset.

Trust in the collective mind of a mass of people who thrive on Love, can change chaos into triumph. This transformation is already well on its way to establishing roots.

Energy, the Basis for Trust

The legitimacy of trust is based on the interaction of energy systems: thought energy, emotional energy and physical energy. Trust is a pattern in which we think, feel, and enact alignment.

YOUR RADIANT BODY, the companion book to this volume, clearly states that "thoughts and emotions create an invisible bridge for change." This is as true in the individual health states, which undergird trust, as in every circumstance of life right down the way through local environment and on to global alignment.

Trust Begins With You

A small treasured book in my library, AS A MAN THINKETH, by James Allen, explains in simple, precise language, the matter of trust:
> Man is buffeted by circumstances so long as he believes himself to be the creature of outside conditions, but when he realizes that he is a creative power, and that he may command the hidden soil and seeds of his being out of which circumstances grow, he then becomes the rightful master of himself.

Start by trusting yourself. And then know that We the People make up the trust of the community, the nation, the world. Individual thought processes are the substance of the collective mass. So what you and I trust is significant to total change. That brings the responsibility right down to where it should be. Do we trust the impact of good, or do we trust violence because it is so widely touted in daily news communication?

Radiant Living in making the clarion call to recognize good beyond evil, or even the good that sometimes evolves from evil, works in partnership with the Hierarchy of Wisdom and Love.

Radiant Living works in partnership with the Hierarchy of Wisdom and Love because it recognizes that Spirit works through human energy. Spirit penetrates thought energy with seeds of love. Wisdom is the guiding force. Wisdom in its quiet power interprets new age thoughts whenever man or woman is geared to trust.

In thoughtful assessment we see that excessive worry — prolonged worry — can only destroy. It destroys the individual. Worry has no berth in ultimate progress, individually or collectively. It has no berth where Infinite Wisdom and Infinite Love are allowed into human understanding.

There are many like James Allen who believe the theory of trust esoterically. And you and I can be two of those, starting now. If we choose! It is a matter of trust that our life's situation can change. Trust self, so that we may see trust prosper in all of life. Until we trust self, we cannot trust another.

Allow the Seeds of Trust to Blossom

I know of a young man who at one point in his life allowed deceit and negligence to corrupt his mindset. He lost his credible job, was left without substance to feed and sustain his beginning family. This well educated man finally took a job as a janitor of an institution, a job he saw as despicable and degrading. In essence it reflected just how he felt about himself. It was in fact an honest job, worthy of honest pay and in no way a demeaning occupation. It was demeaning only in the sense that he made it so in his belief system. After a year or more of his struggle, during which time his loved ones constantly prayed he would understand the depths of his self-made circumstances, he finally did understand through a spectacular shift into a new age of thought for him.

What happened was that at the time when he was ready to accept it, there appeared a part time job in his profession. Still unsure of this new belief system, he hung onto the janitorial duties, working the two jobs. At length he was heard to say, like the prodigal son coming home to himself, "I'm through cleaning latrines." In effect he was saying, "I'm through with my own sense of degradation."

The climb out was a long slow crawl on a path that had all the barriers he had put in place when he allowed that path to deceit. Worry was relentless in challenging his new-found trust, and the lessons he learned in obliterating barrier after barrier were phenomenal. But those lessons learned built an honest path to success, and he would forever remember his slogan, "I'm through cleaning latrines," or effectively translated, "I'm through with deceit." In a sense, they served as valuable affirmations to cleanse the subconscious mind.

Trust Verified Scientifically

The good news for worriers, which in varying degrees includes all of us, is that trust enacted in the mental and emotional energy process can be verified scientifically today. This is especially good news for the logical, left-brain oriented person. It relates to the hard science of research. Going back to the energy systems, we may relate to the interaction of thoughts and emotions with their impact on the physical body. These three energies are involved in the physiology of the nervous system, interacting with the endocrine glands, which produce the hormones according to the direction of the brain as the executor of the nervous system. Not to be intimidated by that seemingly involved and scientific statement, the gist of its meaning is that as you think, so your body reacts physically. And taking it a step farther, the nervous system and the endocrine glands impact directly upon the immune system. The immune system, as you may recognize, is the guardian of your health. Your overall state of well being flourishes when you are free from pain and disease.

In recent years there is constant research in this area of stress related health. And all of it contributes solidly to trust as the antidote of worry. One example is the psychoneuroimmunology research conducted by Candace Pert, Ph.D., at Johns Hopkins University laboratory in Baltimore, Maryland. Pert did her research as Chief of Brain Biochemistry, Clinical Neuroscience Branch, at the National Institute of Mental Health. It relates to the study of neuropeptides, produced by the brain (executor of the nervous system) and the specificity of their receptors within the nervous system.

Her study is an extension of on-going understanding in this field. It enlarges on similar documented material written in some detail in YOUR RADIANT BODY, Chapter II. It is the psychoneuroimmunology theory that explains the interaction of body/mind/feelings. This holistic approach to life in its entire scope of living is one of the exciting changes alternately challenged by the skeptical, yet at the same time quite clearly understood and accepted by a mass mindset of new age people who ultimately trust.

In brief, what Dr. Pert relates to is the hard (verifiable) science of the activity of neuropeptides and their receptors. She explains that there are 50 to 60 neuropeptides, which have previously been called hormones, already identified as manufactured by the brain, and received by the brain- and body-based receptors which activate significant electro-chemical processes within the body. The result speaks to the control one has over circumstances leading either to health or illness through mental and emotional energy.

When I began presenting these concepts in my first Radiant Living Workshop in July, 1977, this research material was somewhere on the leading edge of our culture. Today, great advances are being made. My well founded hope is that by the turn of the century, the holistic pattern incorporated in the psychoneuroimmunology concept will become mainstream. We have in it a promising link with Infinite Wisdom. The truth is the truth is the truth, and you and I, and all humanity, may well get on with the awareness of the truth. In that challenge is the power to heal the world. It is holism in experience, at its zenith.

Holism is practiced by people who choose to be in charge of their lives. Through trust they effectively manifest health and wholeness in all areas of their lives. These will be people like you and me who no longer subscribe to the priesthood of any class of people — in this case, the medical to whom we traditionally abdicate our own health responsibility. New age truth demonstrates that each of us has the responsibility for health.

Undisputably, each one of us is in charge of the remarkable body we live within. We can renew and sustain a remarkable degree of wellness simply at will. Yet "simply" is not as simple as it sounds. In this case, it is the simple application of the profound truth that you and I are what we think in terms of negatives as destructive, or positives as constructive to health and general well being.

I would not dare to write about this in such definite tones if I did not know it from experience. When I was in psychosomatic pain midway through my current life span, I tried to put all the responsibility for diagnosing and treating my pain in the doctors' hands. There were opinions by several doctors before I finally terminated that fruitless quest which found no malfunction, no disease, no malady in my body. An unbalanced nervous system from undue stress does not easily release its picture as the culprit of pain. Yet stress, I finally found, was the problem.

When I put *trust* to the test, I found an abundance of Wisdom and Love coming from the Power we call God. The experience of that Power was the treatment which diminished my pain. Through *trust* I began to see that it was I — not the doctor — who must treat my body. Through *trust* in Infinite Wisdom I began to see that "I am in charge of my own healing." I am the healer because I know where I hurt and how much. No one is as cognizant of my discomfort as I am. As long as it continues, I am the one who must endure it. As a part of that self healing, I experimented with diet and with physical activity. *Trust* led to experimentation, and gradually physical relief encouraged deeper and deeper *trust*.

"Listen to your body," was what Wisdom told me. "Monitor your own pattern of pain." I learned the inevitable fact that I could expect healing in my body commensurate with the healing of mind and feelings — removing the barriers.

Healing is the difference between these two affirmations: 1) "I am healed by the Power of God invested in me at birth," and 2) "God, won't you please heal me? Nevertheless, if this be my cross, I shall bear it bravely (as a martyr)."

The latter is the beggar who does not know (or cannot accept) that he/she already lives within the healing power. The analogy is the person with a million dollar bank account who continues homeless and starving.

A List of Worry One-Liners

Worry is so prevalent in our culture, so pervasive that it tends to seriously undermine trust. We need to look at it as if through a microscope. When we do this creatively, we find a stimulating list of one-liners which may serve to prod the turn-around:
1) Worry is not to be confused with valid concern which alerts us to a specific precaution or direction to take.
2) Excessive concern, on the other hand, builds into worry.
3) Worry wastes, or debilitates energy; individual energy is limited and Wisdom urges the wise use of it.
4) To worry is to abdicate control to chance, like a high speed motor vehicle hitting an expanse of ice.

5) Worry is too logical to fit into new age patterns of *trust*.
6) Worry is too illogical to be practical.
7) Worry is too heavy a load; learn to travel light.
8) Worry is individual choice.
9) Worry is not instinctual; worry is programmed by fear.
10) Worry is the downside of *trust*.
11) Worry is countered by the education provided by the facts of Radiant Living.
12) Worry! Who needs it?

In Summary

Trust is the significant word in any summary of worry. Trust stands on its own merit. Trust feeds on, builds on trust. And what develops is constructive action.

Weigh that good news against the opposite role of worry. All that can be verified as truth for trust in the constructive manifestation, can also be verified as truth for worry in the destructive manifestation. As long as one holds tightly to worry, the barrier it creates will upset life's experience.

Richard Bach says in ILLUSIONS, The Adventures of a Reluctant Messiah, "Argue for your limitations, and sure enough they're yours."

It seems like one of life's cruel hoax that the person who most needs trust to set his/her life in balance, is the one whose inflexibility will not allow it.

Richard Bach has also written in his handbook, "Imagine the universe beautiful and just and perfect." In Radiant Living, this is the perfect visualization.

Many in Radiant Living come back again and again for consultation. They are the ones who sense that trust is a good-news factor for them and for the world. Usually they are not able to completely trust at their first confrontation with worry. But they get ahold of trust piece by piece and the more they get results, the more they allow trust to influence their life. They allow it because trust stands on its own merit in the experience of commanding change in their circumstances.

On the other hand, those who come once, and in their debt of doubt never return, are acting out the jaded response to life: "Trust? So what else is new?" It is their ho-hum attitude that picks up and is strengthened by vibrations from the many in our societal environment who believe that the only way to change for the good is through the sheer effort to pull themselves up by their own bootstraps. In as much as change involves discipline, tugging at the bootstraps is a start. But beyond that is the undeveloped area of serendipity, in which trust tends to open doors hitherto unrecognized and seemingly bolted shut. Serendipity places you and me into the right place at the right time. It is also known as being in the flow.

Trust as it is the antidote for worry cures that dis-ease so that the barrier is effectively banished. Trust allows the flow of Wisdom and Love to heal body as well as circumstances. Long range, trust will heal our world, and make of it a beautiful planet of Love. Let's make a pact to believe in trust.

CHAPTER THREE

Anger and Fear, Barriers to Radiant Living

Excessive Anger and Fear are like a vice seriously restricting Radiant Living. If you choose to practice Radiant Living, the vice voluntarily loosens and your life begins to flow.

Radiant Living is a commitment. It is a lifestyle, a process which in its development invites commitment. The commitment is to purity which allows change and enhances individual awareness of Infinite Wisdom and Infinite Love.

In clarification, Infinite Wisdom explains to the mind how to utilize the Power of Infinite Love in daily living. Thus these two factors become the treatment in the change which seeks purity in place of excessive Anger and Fear.

Infinite Wisdom and Infinite Love as partners demonstrate through human energy as Radiance. This is the Spirit Hierarchy at work, seeking an outlet through those who are "Building and Bridging"* as the "New Group of World Servers."* All of this marks the transition into the 21st Century, often called the New Age.

*"Building and Bridging" is a booklet issued by the School of Esoteric Studies, Suite 1903, 40 E. 49th Street, New York, 10017. It speaks of the "New Group of World Servers." All of this material relates to the Alice A. Bailey books.

Love in its broadest reach has the power to heal. Its potential goes beyond any medical prognosis because regardless of the problem, the Love treatment contributes to the healing process. Today many more are listening to the Love rhetoric but still are only timidly tapping into it. Perhaps change will come with trust in the 21st Century.

Stop! Think about Love as Power. Think about Love as compassion, caring, nurturing and supporting others in their moments of need. But think about it first as that essence which permeates the energy of your own Body, Mind and Feelings. Think about Love as energy with physiological impact, for research conclusively shows that Love enhances the Body's well being at the cellular level.

When you can believe this brand of Love Power, risk it as an experience in your own situation. Let Love happen: "I am aware of Love revitalizing every cell of my Body." Later we'll talk about how it works scientifically, but for starters just trust that your change in attitude will produce change within the temple of your Body. Repeat the above stated affirmation aloud; do so with conviction as often as it comes to mind. Repetition reenforces the memory tract. And as the memory recalls, it strengthens the demonstration of purity within your life.

The Power of Memory in Demonstration

I would like to share with you a poignant personal experience of the power of memory to demonstrate what it dwells upon:

For too long a time, I had given anger the power for my survival. That was in my early thirties. I was angry because of fear. What was I afraid of? My fear was that I would not survive to see myself free from the set of circumstances that seemed to stretch into endless moments of distressed anxiety. In my memory I was saturated with yesterday's anger, which seemed to flow endlessly into today's anger. It was becoming a chronic pattern, and what paralyzed my ability to cope with today, was that I lived in fear of what tomorrow would bring. Coping mostly meant tears of anger and then retaliation toward those I blamed for my circumstances.

One night in the midst of that dark period of my life, I had a dream. Before I awoke from it, I was standing on the edge of the blackest of pits. You cannot share my experience in full detail unless you, too, have stood there at the brink of your own blackest of pits. I hope you have not, for it is a feeling of desolation beyond words to describe.

When I awoke from that dream, I "flew" out of bed, ran to the living room and turned on the brightest light, many lights all around me. The only reality I knew was the need to escape that blackest of pits. If I fell in, it was all over!

Light came to me, there in that artificial lamp light. That Light was undeniably the Power of Love. In that mental dawning, my entire body quivering, the panic that had reduced my oxygen supply and left me faint was released. With that panic-release, I sat in reality, knowing I was in the safety of my living (a Love) room, extremely relieved that the "blackest of pits" was but a hallucination, albeit emotionally induced. In my innate sensitivity, I had a sense of being surrounded by Spirit Guides.

I sat there until daybreak, as I recall, gathering into my knowing — from Infinite Wisdom — that I was not alone. My fear dissipated, my quivering body became stable, and I resolved to find a way out of this secret, intense morass of anxiety. The surge of relief in the hour or two that followed, made clear the message that I must be responsible as the liberator in this life drama of circumstances. Up to now, I had chosen the bit part, submissive to the "star" (in my mind) of my circumstances. At that time, submissiveness was the only role I knew. Now within the Light I saw the creation of a new role. And Spirit would direct this new script. The isolation I had long *imagined* in my dilemma was simply that. Now was the time for change; I would take charge of my life. I suppose the full impact of that mandate did not hit me at once, or I would have been overwhelmed. But what I know for sure, and remember these many years later, is that this magnificent realization was every bit of it a product of my enlightenment from the Power of Love surrounding me in my moment of desperate need.

Within the significant period of months that followed, the old pattern of frequent tears diminished. I learned to stand tall in my gratitude for the Good that was happening. My very sanity had been salvaged by Love Power, and I had accepted the most difficult role of my lifetime: stop relating anger in response to the anger around me; instead, return Love for anger. At first it was all hazy and undefined. For a while I was saying "yes" and "no" at the same time. Did you know that scenario was possible? Well, it is. It is the battle between enlightenment and the lesser power of human logic. Human logic kept asking, "Why should I be the one to change?" The answer from Infinite Wisdom was that someone had to change, and "you can only control your own life." The beautiful result, anyone knows who has accepted that script, is that usually the change of one person ripples out into change of the other(s), to whatever degree.

In attitude change it is the subconscious that is hard to convince. This, again, is where the affirmation process directs the computer/mind's printout. The one I used repeatedly at that time, and still do frequently: "I am free from the irritations of the moment." Play that back to yourself and see the logic of it, which is why it works. It means I must detach, remembering that I do not have to react with anger to every little ruffle. It means I must act responsibly in rebuffing what previously, for such a long time, had aroused my anger. Ultimate freedom means that many demands have been fulfilled, but even when freedom seems to be won, it is only relative to the circumstances of the moment. Freedom has to be reworked every day for every change in one's life.

Pitirim A. Sorokin, An Apostle of Love

Pitirim A. Sorokin has written that "Man's freedom lies in his ability to cultivate his greatest source of creative and regenerative power." For many years I have had in my file Dr. Sorokin's treatise on "The Mysterious Energy of Love." It came into my hands during those early years of change. It came to me from the Reverend Dr. Cecil Murrow of Iowa. In this significant paper, Dr. Sorokin speaks of the need to explore the scientific realm of the mysterious domain of altruistic love. I believe he made this pioneering proposal as early as the 1930s. At the time his colleagues ridiculed his theory — they could not understand what he was saying. Quite likely they had never known Love as he did in his survival from many of life's rejections.

Who was Dr. Sorokin? He was born in Russia, and studied at the University of St. Petersburg. He was a member of the Constituent Assembly under the Kerensky regime and subsequently suffered imprisonment by the Communists. When he was at last freed he resumed his studies at the University of St. Petersburg only to be banished shortly thereafter by the Soviet government. At that time he came to the United States. In 1930 he was invited to become chairman of the Sociology Department at Harvard University, where he continued to work for the rest of his life. In 1948 he established the Harvard Research Center in Creative Altruism. He died in February 1968.

The Radiance of Infinite Wisdom which set me free within the Power of Infinite Love is Dr. Sorokin's altruistic love at work in the universe. It salvaged, at once, my sanity so that it could work through me to salvage other lives as well. It coaxed me into and is still directing my efforts in this global work of health and wholeness and right relationships. Altruistic love is working through human energy in the lives of people all over the world. Perhaps it is, or will be, working through your life. None of us are "chosen" people as such; we are people who have chosen of our own initiative to responsibly discipline our lives so that we may become catalysts for Good.

Radiant Living Workshops

In the Radiant Living Program some of our most intense workshop sessions dealt with the experience of confronting Anger and Fear. We decided to capitalize the two words because they are significant entities which must be addressed. The two seem to have been invited at various times into the life of each of us as we maneuvered our own sophistication within this society of blatant violence and hatred. This is a society where we often have to struggle for survival.

As the presenter and catalyst for Radiant Living Workshops, I brought a skeleton of thought which the participants were invited to tie into, giving their own energy to develop a practical pattern for inspiring group enlightenment. The intense energy projected from these many different personalities brought out the following selected thoughts:

Our basic premise was that there is:
1) A Power greater than I am individually. That Power is God. Or it could be called Universal Life Energy, Infinite Mind, Mother Earth...
2) I am a part of that Power (Energy). I do not exist within a vacuum; I do not exist in isolation. Nor is that Power encapsulated within a space shut apart from me.
3) As a part of that Power, I am part of you, for you, too, are a part of that Power (Energy).
4) I believe because I *trust*. In my finite mind and with my finite vocabulary I cannot fully understand nor explain it. I am comfortable in summarizing it very simply, yet profoundly:

GOD IS; I AM; YOU ARE. All belong to the Oneness of Life. All are energy units of this Oneness.

Radiant Living as a Way of Life:
Radiant Living as a Way of Life is woven from the constant practice of Wisdom and Love. It accepts change as part of the process.

Radiant Living as a program of mutual enrichment, both gives and receives.

Radiant Living both radiates and attracts.

Radiant Living makes it possible to create any desired circumstance.

Radiant Living is a constant discipline.

Radiant Living acknowledges that:
1) There is Order in the Universe.
2) Spiritual Laws are operating and are valid because of that Order.
3) Order within my life as a person, brings me into alignment with overall Order and Spiritual Law.
4) Therefore, like the analogy of sowing and reaping: As I believe (plant seeds), so will I demonstrate (harvest).

Trust as a factor of Prime Awareness: (We used the following as affirmations.)
"I AM AWARE OF GOD IN EVERY CELL OF MY BODY."
"I AM AWARE OF GOD IN EVERY CELL OF THE UNIVERSE."
"I AM AWARE OF GOD EXPRESSING THROUGH MY HUMAN ENERGY."
"I AM A SIGNIFICANT LIFE WITHIN THE ORDER OF THE UNIVERSE."

The individual belief system is extremely important in Radiant Living:
1) To believe is to recognize a process in action, a process which flows as constant change.
2) To believe is to accept the whole because of understanding the parts: Body, Mind and Feelings — physical energy, mental energy, and emotional energy. All are combined as factors within the spiritual entity.
3) Yet belief without action is stagnant. ASK is the significant link between belief, or trust, and demonstration. Graphically it looks like this:

A S K (And it shall be given)   Taken from
S eek (And you shall find)   Biblical Wisdom
K nock (And the door will open)   Matthew 7:7

ASK is the keyword. Spiritual Law demands that you will have an answer when you ask with honest intent. It is a human fallacy to blunder through life without asking specifically, without a goal, or a commitment.

SEEK is the natural sequence to ASKing. It means discipline, persistence, meaningful pursuit, visualizing what you want or the experience you want to happen.

KNOCK is synonymous with knowing that the "door" will open for you to enter.

An Experience of Infinite Wisdom and Infinite Love

Perhaps an episode in the life of one of our workshop participants will explain the effectiveness of ask and believe. We'll call her Mary. She lived with a husband who seemed to unleash his anger at the slightest provocation. During a sharing session within a nurturing setting, Mary explained to workshop participants that in his demonstration her husband frequently cursed loudly. He never displayed any physical violence; nevertheless, the verbal violence created emotional devastation for her.

We encouraged Mary to ASK of Infinite Wisdom, in meditative sessions, how she should receive her husband's Anger. Within her silence it came through to Mary, clearly expressed: "The Power of Love — activate it."

Mary had participated in the rhetoric of Love Power as we had discussed it at length in our sessions. Now in meditation, in the silence of her mind, she was clearly being asked to express Love in action.

"Love? when I'm being cursed at in foul terms by a man who becomes a monster?" she asked tearfully.

The answer was smooth and implicit: "Simply see him wrapped in Infinite Love."

So she determined to try it during her next confrontation with him at home. In the action experience, Mary was surprised to discover that she and her husband were both wrapped in Infinite Love. She had a difficult time explaining just how she knew, but there was a strange vibratory heat she could feel. She felt so overwhelmed by that Infinite Love, that she recalled being quite oblivious to the cursing after the initial outburst which brought her to claim Love. "There we were," she said in tears, "in a mutual bond of Infinite Love. I don't know what Sam felt; he didn't share it. Maybe he wasn't fully aware of it, but the cursing episode, as I remember it, suddenly stopped."

Her first report to the workshop support group was fantastic. Those who already had evoked the Power of Love at some point in their lives cried and hugged Mary in understanding. Others who lived in similar jeopardy, awaiting a solution, not daring to try the treatment, first sat in awe, then stood and joined the "celebration" of Mary's Infinite Love treatment. Infinite Love simply waits for us to ASK.

Mary's sharing electrified our evening's session. It was a success story that actually was well orchestrated in terms of awakening her awareness leading up to the treatment. Yet it was phenomenal to all those who had only accepted Love in dribbles. In subsequent Love-wrap treatments, Mary reported that she turned away from her husband in silence — just removing herself physically from his presence during his disruptive behavior. In effect she was ignoring him, temporarily, so that she could maintain her equilibrium.

There came a point in the weeks beyond that first glorious experience when she began to feel alienation from him. "Maybe the scenes are fewer and farther between," she said to me one day in consultation, "but they are still happening." Infinite Love had helped her to feel less devastated, but she admitted that she was more lax in evoking the Love treatment for Sam. "I care less about his plight," she said, especially since she had approached him in one of his stable moments, and tried to talk about his cursing habit at the slightest provocation. He would have no part of a discussion.

As the months went by, she knew they were being held together in a bond of Infinite Love. But her own sense of alienation from him increased as far as her bonded love with him. She no longer felt it meaningful to be anything more than at peace with herself, no matter how he acted. Yes, there was a change in him, a kind of mellowing in actions toward her, but the cursing seemed to be his own right. As we shared, she was adamant that it was his problem: "Let him work it out; I'm tired." All the while she was giving a great deal of energy to the larger cause of holding onto Infinite Wisdom and Infinite Love in all her life's experiences. Mary was growing apart from Sam who was being left behind in his snarled life.

One day she came to me in somewhat of a panic: "I don't want this separation to happen," she said. What to do about it?

She and I joined in a meaningful meditation so that she could call upon the Power of Love to give her an answer. It came through: "Attach your fleeting love to Infinite Love." It came complete with the graphics in which she saw a memo (her love) stapled to a Love treatise (Infinite Love). In her visualization she rolled it up and put it in the chute, the old pneumatic tube-way in which stores used to handle messages to another department (before computers).

She determined to enhance that visualization by rehearsing it daily until the next angry cursing episode with her husband. When put to the test, it worked.

Of course it worked. It worked now, whereas before it had failed, because now she was putting a great deal of energy into its manifestation. "It was," she explained, "as if the lesser love (her own) caught fire from being attached to Infinite Love which she was now actively calling upon to help her. As a result, their own love bond became stronger than it had been for years.

When she came to care for Sam once again, she went a step farther. She risked reprimanding him, feeling secure about doing so. "If you must swear, get lost. Get out of my sight and hearing. I'm offended by your swearing, and I'm not going to listen to it." At that point she would calmly go about her business, holding her ground, expecting him to go away. In her own way she pointed the way to Love in response to his Anger. Gradually, when there was no forum for his ventilating Anger, he learned to curb it. Sometimes he would curse under his breath, Mary reported. At least he was trying to change. The true solution could have been for him to be courageous enough to confront the reason for his anger. What was happening between Mary and Sam, at least for her, was a marital triumph. Since Sam never did confront his Anger he is probably still carrying it — let's say it has gone underground. But that is his problem and Mary doesn't concern herself with what she cannot change. Through the change that she could control in her own life, the marriage took a more stable relationship for both of them.

Anger In Its Many Faces

As other workshop participants shared their similarly meaningful experiences, we tried to understand Anger in its many faces. It was a real challenge, the more so because we worked at it collectively. So many good ideas came forth. The following material is how we finally left it, after many additions and deletions. We agreed there was much more to say about Anger, but that it could never all be said if we were to try for concise, clear statements:

ANGER IS ENERGY:
  If Constructive Anger, it is energy well used.
  If Destructive Anger, it is energy squandered.
A) Constructive Anger — Anger as a Warning Signal
  1) Honest confrontation between two or more people with the intent of saying all the things on their minds, concerning a central problem between them. Those involved either consciously or subconsciously realize that this angry exchange has a purpose, that of bringing it all out in the open.
  2) In the end, a resolution is reached to be done with the problem. A significant pact is made that there will be no more looking back or rehashing the same thing.
  3) Forgive and forget, through the medium of a Love Treatment, attaching their love to Infinite Love.
  4) Such a confrontation drains the energy, may even give temporary Body discomfort. But it is energy well spent when it achieves the goal.

An example of this Constructive Anger is the occasional episode in the lives of a young couple I know who every now and then go into their basement and shout at each other over the particular problem they cannot resolve in any other way. (Both of them have high Fire count in their astrology charts.) They live in a sheltered setting where their raised voices easily carry to others unless they go to the basement and close the door. This treatment serves for them as a kind of catharsis; they both know what they are doing and it seems to settle the "fire." It is, I suggest, a part of their growth pattern which in time will no longer be needed as they develop more tranquility in their individual lives.

B) Destructive Anger — Chronic Anger
  1) Repeated sessions of Anger, like a drama that adds a new scene every day; same plot, same principal characters in same relationship.
  2) Principals deny their Anger; principals refuse to "own" their Anger. Such as "You make me so angry!" This is the statement which precedes a tirade of angry accusations.
  3) Anger at inanimate objects: **The car won't start** — swear

at it; get out and kick it; slam it in physical violence. **A misplaced letter or bill** — swear at it, use the fist to strike furniture and slam drawers shut. **The traffic light turns red just as the driver approaches the intersection** — The driver is in a big hurry, frustrated because of his/her own late start, so the response is to swear at the situation and pound the steering wheel.

You question these types of responses? Yes, adults with extreme Anger problems do respond in the above manners, even when in other ways they seem stable. Or so it has been reported to me.

C) Second-Hand Anger
   1) Being locked into cursing-angry eruptions of a spouse, business colleague, child, brother/sister, parent. (Any one of a close relationship.)
   2) Decision has to be made by victim whether to act responsibly or whether to re-act with Anger.
   3) Remember that other person "owns" his/her Anger, but the victim "owns" his/her action in response.
      a) Acting in **defense:** allowing oneself to be harassed, returning Anger for Anger.
      b) Developing a viable **offense:** withstanding the tug of emotion to return Anger instead of being in charge with a calm approach; removing oneself from the scene of the cursing-anger and invoking the Infinite Love treatment.

The Dynamics of Anger

Question: What is this thing called Anger that disrupts an otherwise peaceful life? In experience it oftentimes ruins an otherwise beautiful relationship of two caring people whether in a love bonding or professional working relationship.

Answer: We call it sneaky and volatile. We characterize Anger as an entity with a shape of its own. Until we understand it we tend to back away and shake a finger at it as if it were a bad child.

What a cop-out! Realistically, Anger is a personality trait of the person whose energy expresses it. The one who expresses that Anger "owns" it and is responsible for it. The bottom line to Anger is that it is a characteristic of an undisciplined life, whenever it is used to excess.

At first flash, Anger is neutral.

Anger is a warning, a news flash, an alert that an energy-storm is brewing.

The brain as the executor of the Nervous System starts the process of Anger.

Anger is an electro-chemical process within the physical body, calling into play the Nervous System and the Endocrine Gland System. (For a detailed rundown, see pages 27-28, "Stress and Its Toll on the Body," in the companion book, **YOUR RADIANT BODY.**)

When we look at it in all its dimensions, we see that Anger is the thing which precipitates heart attacks, strokes, cancer — disease in general — when it is not adequately resolved.

Anger is one of the emotions that unlocks the door to the memory storehouse, called the subconscious and it can call-up all sorts of fears.

We tend to think we cannot control Anger; we say it is such a sudden, spontaneous energy. We allow ourselves to wallow in the rut that believes: "I was so angry I didn't know what I was doing."

Wrong! If we will research our own Anger, using reflection and meditation, seeing its cause and effect in calm and sane moments, we can stock the memory storehouse or subconscious with thoughts that counteract the habit of exploding in a fit or tantrum of red-hot flash. But the will to discipline is imperative. The person whose energy is being dissipated by Anger has to care about change! The victim cannot do it for the perpetrator.

Affirmations can be very helpful. "When I was a kid I had temper tantrums; now that I am an adult, I deal with destructive emotion in a responsible way."

Technique for Dealing with Anger

Research your own Anger. In deep reflection (meditation) stand apart from it and see what it is all about. Start by admitting that Anger is seriously disrupting your life, in terms of relationships.
In Radiant Living we see Anger in the perspective of Wisdom and Love. The Wisdom to understand it, and the Love to treat it.
Take a phase of your Anger into meditation.
See it as a Thread of your Life.
Get ahold of that Thread and trace it to its source. Is it tied to a Fear?
Does it lead you to a relationship that you are angry about being locked into? Is that the bottom line that is making you angry about many other things in your life? If not a relationship, try other areas of your life.

In working with individuals in private consultation, we use guided imagery sessions. Starting with "the voice" of the facilitator — my voice — we evoke a meditative awareness of tranquility. In that setting, "the voice" guides the individual into an experience of confrontation which is anchored by his/her tranquility of the moment.

Invariably, strategic insight comes, usually symbolically, as the participant is able to view him/herself on stage in a scenario. It is as if he/she were in the audience of a stage play. At the close of the guided imagery scenario, the participant is urged to express the feelings in art work, or to write it out. In sharing those results we piece together the root of that Anger.

It takes more than one mental imagery session. And it takes much determination to free oneself from blatant and recurring Anger. Sometimes the scenario appears similar to a child's temper tantrum, and may in fact be traced to that origin. In an adult, it becomes a temper tantrum acting out the child within. In that realization it needs to be addressed with the responsibility of an adult.

The crucial factor in Anger, its creation and its expression, is that without a victim it has no forum. You are the victim if in encountering another's Anger you respond irresponsibly with your own Anger. You are also the victim as long as you endure or listen to another's angry expression. Risk walking away from that Anger. See what happens. Know that you are worthy of being treated with respect, and that does not include another's indulgence in Anger at your expense.

Fear In Its Many Faces

In a sense, Fear piggy-backs Anger. It goads Anger into expression in cases where it is then the root of Anger.
But in a broader context, Fear is entirely an entitity in its own right. Following are some of the points we considered in our workshop analysis of Fear:

I. **Fear/Fright**
Fear as a sudden fright is an instinctual emotion to imminent danger.

Fear triggers the secretion of a body-drug, the hormone adrenalin from the adrenal glands, which gives physiological impetus for action.

This action encourages the Body's ability to handle the situation of danger or emergency of the moment.

It supplies unusual physical strnegth and/or unusual mental insight.

This is characterized as the fright/flight/fight syndrome.

The late Dr. Hans Selye has given us many insights to the way in which the body handles the stress of fear. He postulated that the body responds to continued stress in three stages which he calls the General Adaptation Syndrome: 1) the **alarm** reaction in which the person becomes aware of the stressor; 2) the stage of **resistance** in which the body adapts to the stressor, and 3) the stage of **exhaustion** in which the body loses its ability to adapt. Beyond this stage, illness usually sets in.

II. **Fear, Past and Future**
Fear has a memory reaction which recalls past experience and rushes on into anticipation of future re-enactment.

For example, driving a vehicle in the rain at near freezing temperature, the driver recalls icy road conditions and anticipates future danger in handling his/her vehicle.

In another example, a person feeling the first touch of a sore throat recalls a strep infection which triggered a long range illness with extreme discomfort. The anticipation of reenactment of that scenario sparks fear/panic which tends to stymie the activation of the immune system in averting a similar situation. In such a case, Fear is working counter to the best interest of that body.

III. Fear, Lack of Self-confidence

This is the chronic Fear that obsesses the person afflicted with low self-image. It is an advanced stage, a deeply ingrained feeling of unworthiness. In my observations during client consultations, this characterizes perhaps as many as eighty-five percent of those in the Fear syndrome.

In a sense it is the root of all Fear: fear that one is not capable of handling one's own life — of not being in charge.

IV. Fear, Feeling of Isolation

This classification is an offshoot of Fear relating to unworthiness.

In low self-esteem, the individual feels unworthy of relationships, fortifies oneself by condoning the "loner" identity.

Healthy functioning of aloneness encourages growth; but obsessive, extreme isolation is neurotic.

The difference between the two is that the neurotic embarks on bizarre behavior.

This bizarre behavior is usually an expression of violent Anger.

It is the Anger which stalks society, brings heinous crimes directed at innocent victims: rape, human mutilation, murder, some form of black magic.

Fear, like Anger, can be constructive or destructive. Like Anger, the effective treatment is meditation wherein Infinite Wisdom explains the appropriate action of Infinite Love. This is another basic tenet of Radiant Living.

As in the confrontation of Anger, the confrontation of Fear is more than the understanding of its meaning and dynamics. Fear requires the treatment of its own appropriate affirmations, such as "I am aware of God in every cell of my Body." Thus I am not alone — not ever. Not in this Body form, nor even when I transcend Body into Spirit.

"I am a significant life within the Law of the Universe." I am here for a purpose.

"I trust the Plan for my life."

And lastly, in the treatment of Fear, as in Anger, ASK is the crucial action.

A S K (And it shall be given)	Taken from
S eek (And you shall find)	Biblical Wisdom
K nock (And the door will open)	Matthew 7:7

In Summary

In summary, Radiant Living is the interaction of body physiology with positive thoughts and stable emotions which transcend excessive Anger and obsessive Fear.

Radiant Living is making responsible choices for maintaining health. Or in the event of illness, it is making responsible choices to enhance healing. Radiant Living discounts panic and suggests the quiet of meditation.

CHAPTER FOUR

Jealousy, What Does It Mean?

When Radiant Living Workshop participants are asked to name some of their personal barriers to harmony, jealousy is rarely mentioned. It is too sly a trait to be recognized. It lurks in the shadows, like the Wicked Witch hovering over children at play. Jealousy is so painful to face.

Quite unknowingly, I harbored jealousy in my life for many years and but for Infinite Wisdom's revelation, I probably never would have dragged it out, kicking and sputtering, from the shadows of my life.

What is the feel of jealousy? Certainly it is not a stable emotion. It is triggered by the subconscious game of making comparisons. It is often linked with the knowing that "I can do better than I am doing. I could achieve more than I have." Jealousy, then, relates to the laid-back power that is not being expressed. The jealous person projects her/himself into the shoes of one who is achieving what she/he would like to achieve, and strongly believes, perhaps subconsciously, that she/he could achieve.

Ultimately, jealousy brings on a dislike for that person who is the achiever at best, and downright hatred and contempt at the extreme. That feeling builds when the achiever ignores the attitude of the jealous person — or if the achiever, as is often the case, is simply insensitive to the under-achiever's problem. This is excusable because it is not the achiever's problem. On the other hand, to be supportive of another with a problem is a bonus potential of those who do achieve. Oftentimes a kind word of encouragement helps another to see, and perhaps solve, an underlying hurt because of the practice of jealousy. And that consideration would be entirely in keeping with Radiant Living.

However, we primarily need to address the problem of the person who owns the jealousy. It is a kind of perverse game. And the person who plays the game is vulnerable until she/he accepts the logic that in the game of life, the players come together as equals with divergent potentials. Within that logic, there is no need for comparison.

People as equals with divergent potentials overrides jealousy because granted that, no one can feel inferior. Everyone has something to give. Cooperation rules out competition. And when people are determined to give whatever it is they have to contribute, they become much too obsessed (used in a positive sense) with working out the good to allow jealousy. They simply do not "hear" the enticement which the entity known as Jealousy offers in its useless philandering.

Start By Owning Your Jealousy

Like Anger, Jealousy must be *owned* by its victim. If you are willing to allow Jealousy to play games with your life, then own up to it and suffer the consequences. What it will attract is the whole Barrier Family which includes Worry, Anger and Fear (members we have already dealt with in previous chapters).

You will Worry about being inadequate when you compare yourself to any of numerous others who have made greater achievements than you have. You will know Anger because someone obviously (in your mind) has so much more going for them than you have yet been able to discipline yourself to achieve. You will even allow Fear to smirch your common sense because you haven't recognized at the moment your potential for the future.

Once you've allowed the Barrier Family to get a toehold, then you have to plan how to dismiss the whole clan. And that is when Jealousy becomes the sly heckler. Every way you turn, whap! another reason to dislike another person. Oh, you won't be heard to say, "You know, I hate Janey (or Johnny) because I'm jealous of her (or him)." No, no; that would be much too blatant a confession. At least that is the way it was for me. I would more likely say, "I don't know what it is about her/him, but I just don't like her/him." I would follow that with a guilt-laugh, and fudge a little if anyone pressed me further on why I didn't like the person.

I could make up all kinds of games when Jealousy was heckling me. I could get angry and make some very unreasonable demand; I could be so afraid, I'd get physically ill, or I could worry when I went to bed instead of sleeping. And when I couldn't sleep, in the morning I was so tired I worked myself into some sort of strange behavior that even baffled me. I was on a vicious treadmill and didn't know how to get off.

Finally, when I was about as uncomfortable as a person could be without completely falling apart, I would come to my old standby: introspection. Later I came to call it relaxation and meditation. And then I was in the flow of Infinite Wisdom and Infinite Love, which in the pattern of Radiant Living brings all the answers.

Wisdom and Love Suggest a New Approach to Jealousy

At that point when I was ready to give up my own game plan (jealousy), Wisdom and Love would suggest a replacement that was much easier to handle: See myself in Love, first; and then move into that other's space and see both of us in Love. With the Radiance that follows, there comes the ultimate change. Jealousy is gone. Jealousy doesn't even try to flaunt perverse charm when Radiance appears.

When Jealousy knows it is defeated, it gathers together the whole Barrier Family, ready to bow out, and they whisk away to hide in the wings until the curtain goes up once again and they are free to frisk and heckle at the next scene.

The way I see it, we make our choice. Members of the Barrier Family visit by invitation only. And you and I issue that invitation. Where one member is invited, the whole family usually squeezes in; they are that closely aligned.

It would be redundant to say more about Jealousy, for its tricks are similar to the other members of the Barrier Family. And the techniques which encourage Jealousy to withdraw are much the same.

In Summary

The summarizing statement is to "know oneself." Discipline oneself to use the high road, not with a holier-than-thou, onerous pattern, but know and discipline oneself because of the great long-range merit.

I like feeling comfortable about me. Fragmentation or frustration? I don't need them in my life. I've tasted enough to know how sour that pattern can be. In cooperation, striving for the highest in my own potential, I have much to give in healing this world. So do you.

CHAPTER FIVE

Order in the Universe

In Radiant Living we stand firmly on the premise that there is Order in the Universe. We acknowledge that Spiritual Laws operate and are valid because of that Order, and conversely that Order has created the Laws.

Further, we know that Order within the individual's life as the microcosm brings alignment with Order and Spiritual Law in the grand scheme of the macrocosm. Therefore, like the Biblical analogy of sowing and reaping: As I believe (plant), so will I demonstrate (harvest).

Desire and Discipline in the Discovery of Order

Order in the Universe sounds nebulous and grandiose until we look at it as if through a microscope. What does Order mean in the individual's life?

We start by saying that you have freewill to accept or reject Order as a Power in your life. After that, remember that daily choices are vital. Each choice you make either promotes Order or it condones chaos.

What is your intent for this very day you prepare to begin? Is it your intent to know peace with all you meet, and to serve the Order of the Universe in every way utilizing your potential?

If so, you will greet the day with both a smile that is apparent by the pleasant look on your face, and in the inner "smile" of your mental and emotional attitude. Prepare your thoughts and emotions to be positive and stable. Even so it is highly possible that inconsequentials will beset you for all your good intent early in the day. So prepare, also, to meet that eventuality. Even as we talked earlier about the importance of the subconscious in resolution of excessive worry, and anger and fear, know it is important to direct the subconscious now to track with your conscious intent of high purpose for your day, come what may.

What is the best way to direct the subconscious? Once again, affirmations are very effective. In this case we suggest from our Radiant Living workshop experience: I am free from the irritations of inconsequentials.

Let's cite an example of what we mean by inconsequential: It is a factor such as a significant person for you — at home or at work or at a volunteer spot where you are serving — acting by nature in just the opposite way of your intent for the day. Suppose that other person has a great anger to express, and it spills out onto you.

This undeniably presents a challenge and every challenge is particularly stimulating, so see what you can make of it. Start with the mental repetition of your affirmation which categorizes the other person's anger as inconsequential. To look at this situation in depth, if the person wants to talk about his/her anger and is reasonable in seeking some input from you for a solution, you may be able to give some healthy suggestions. At least you will be more able to understand the person's needs if you maintain the "smile" you started with at the onset of your day. We're speaking here primarily of your mental attitude. Serving where you are asked for input is part of the intent for Good.

If you cannot help, meaning the other person does not want a solution, but only wants to flaunt anger — is not ready to be anything but openly disagreeable — then the other person's anger, or whatever it may be, is surely inconsequential in your day's intent. So rely again on your affirmation: I am free from the irritations of inconsequentials. In terms of seeking Order in your immediate universe, you may determine, and rightly so, to detach from that problem over which you have no jurisdiction. Just allow that other person to own that anger, and you ignore it.

When you determine to accept Order, and truly persevere in that determination, you will move forward in like manner throughout the day. All of this presents an immense challenge. See how many days you can continue this worthy intent without breaking the discipline of it.

There are, of course, many factors which deter us from our individual pusuit of Order. Within the setting of our Radiant Living workshops, participants list things that upset their own sense of Order. And always we list these things with the reminder that we have freewill to correct or to ignore the correction of these factors.

Included in the participants' listings were some very simple things, like a picture on the wall or a lampshade being out of kilter. Yes, we are talking about seemingly inconsequentials which can be upsetting at least to the subconscious.

Physical clutter was included on the majority of the lists. Sometimes this included a child's or a spouse's continual clutter. Being subjected to someone else's disarray makes for a more difficult solution, but it, too, may be handled judiciously using the Radiant Living basics of Wisdom and Love. There is usually clutter of one's own to deal with first. And often the example of cleaning up that helps to alleviate the family problem.

Clutter Creates Chaos

I can easily recall the impact of clutter in my own life. There was a portion of my kitchen counter that held all the immediate debris of grocery shopping trips and daily cooking chores — so many items of clutter it would take pages to list. In my pattern of growth I came to realize that I could clear the top drawer below the kitchen counter and use it to hold those items I needed to salvage. The drawer would hold only so much, so I had to sort out and save only the necessary. At that time I had plenty of clutter to sort out in my life, and a big part of it was the physical substance disarray. The pleasant thing is to remember how good I felt every time I put an area of my house in order.

There came into my life later in those years of growth, a dear friend whom I shall call Eppie. She was the mother of a friend my daughter discovered during her freshman year away at college. Whenever Eppie came through Des Moines on her way to visit her daughter at college, she had an open invitation to stay with us overnight. Sometimes she arrived unexpectedly. The first time that happened, I apologized for the clutter in the room where she would sleep, saying "This room catches all the extras we don't take time to put away immediately."

She laughed long and raucously, befitting her amiable nature and large carriage. "You don't know what clutter is until you've seen my house," she said forthrightly.

The first time I visited her — even with afore notification — I saw what she meant. Here was the original, the full-blown clutter-nest. As we entered Eppie's home, a table in the hallway had newspapers stacked precariously beyond description or comprehension. If someone had inadvertently side-swiped the table in passing, they would have been, for sure, inundated with newsprint. And that was only the beginning. The motif in every room in her home could aptly have been described as disarray. From her own previous account she knew her home was cluttered, but she obviously chose to live with it.

How had this affected her life? It was true to the paraphrased universal law that where there is no order, chaos reigns. Eppie had endured for years a particularly hectic marriage that produced a daughter (our daughter's friend) and a son. Finally came a most unpleasant divorce. But that not until she had attracted a near life-shattering accident that left her crippled even though fully mobile. "Thank God for mobility, at any rate," she said many times over as she shared her past. The high note is that none of it seemed to thwart her fiercely independent nature or exceptional will to live and persevere. She went on to complete her master's degree academically, and to move into a highly responsible job. The fact is her entire life was an example of how clutter does detract from harmony in one's life. The physical clutter was only the outward manifestation of disorganization in thoughts and emotions.

This does not mean that there is necessarily visible clutter whenever tragedy occurs. But it does mean that being surrounded by extreme clutter undeniably contributes to a mental attitude which attracts life's imbalances. Those who argue otherwise are simply unaware of the validity of Spiritual Laws.

The fact is that physical clutter creates mental clutter which is the real barrier to harmony. We have only to clear out and set in order a drawer or a closet or an entire room, and then take particular note of how good we feel. Or look in the mirror and discover that the furrowed brow has disappeared — maybe even the smile of self approval has arrived. When you have done a long-neglected cleaning job, go to the mirror and smile at yourself; it is a way of saying "thank you" to the person you are.

Our Radiant Living Workshop discussions on the subject of clutter frequently led us to note that one person's clutter can be another's treasure. Going back to Eppie's home, her clutter by my appraisal (not judgement) quite likely was her treasure. I can equate that in some degree with my own office room in our home. It is my domain. It is one place where others would often get the feeling of excessive clutter. The biggest reason is that I clip newsstories in great volume. I do so that I will have the significant events of days and weeks and months at hand for my writing. Periodically I walk into my office and know it is time to sort out some of those clippings. This comes at a time when they seem to be taking over the whole room. I keep them filed in folders by subject matter, but the time comes when some of the clippings are so old they can be trashed. My cursory evaluation of Eppie's newspaper stack reminded me even at that time of how easily one can be inundated by newsprint; we probably both have a mutual attachment to the printed word.

Garden Weeds as Clutter

My husband Don and I have had a small garden patch

somewhere at the edge of our lawn in every home we've owned. Even when we moved into a condominium complex, Don came in one day delighted to have found a garden plot for us across the street and down the block a ways. My own reaction was complete dismay. I was the one with the farmer heritage. He was a city-kid. And I had long ago worn out my need to have a garden. I knew so well the discipline of pulling weeds. I knew it went on all season long. To Don the garden meant the excitement of choosing seeds to plant, getting them "quickly and easily" into the ground. No such thing for him of staking out strings to guide straight rows. If it was a dry summer season, he watered quite regularly, but the rest of a garden meant waiting for harvest.

Weeds were inconsequential to Don, and he refused to be irritated by them. On the other hand, from my farm training weeds were clutter and chaos for me. I suppose that pattern could be, in the final analysis, a throw-back to the pigweed that grew so profusely and so tall on our farm. It was never a part of our garden, it never got a toehold in that well tended area. With Dad's tutelage, his six children never let that happen. But the south side of my beautiful hill, spoken of earlier, leveled down to the corn crib and pigpen and every growing season it was covered with the ugliness of pigweed. As a child I always thought the pigs had some direct bearing on the pigweed. At any rate, that pigweed towered well above the smaller clutter of weeds that seemed to grow undisturbed on that south hill. Everyone of us was so busy with our garden weeding and numerous other farm chores that we pretended not to see the hill. At long last we would get the edict from Dad to "get at that pigweed."

In my imaginative, child's mind I used to think each time it was my turn to attack the problem, "Why don't you just go away? No one plants you; no one wants you." If rejection by a child's mind could have any impact on a plant, that pigweed would never have had a chance. The hardest part was to try to get the roots, for as Dad always pointed out, "Get the roots and maybe we can destroy it." But obviously we didn't do a very good job of that, for every summer it was back in the same habitat. By the time we got it hacked down, it was so overgrown that we had to drag it off to the brushpile to be burned. The smaller weeds just withered into compost. The lesson: clutter temporarily ignored grows into ever greater confusion and wasted time.

But now after all these years of remembering pigweed as clutter on our farm, I recently read an article from the Associated Press with the headline: "Pigweed Joins the Ranks of Health Foods." What? One person's clutter is another's good health?

"Farmers curse and chop it. Poets and Indians have immortalized it. And now health food stores are selling it."

In fact, when I introduced the subject of pigweed and our memories of it as children into a recent conversation with my two older sisters, our brother-in-law told us his mother had indeed cooked the leaves as greens when he was a boy.

Pigweed, it seems, is but one of more than fifty species of the plant life called amaranth. Today it is being made into flour as a viable alternative for those who are allergic to gluten in regular flour. Its lore goes back at least five hundred years. The Aztec Indians used it as a main food source, we are told. They also attributed "special powers" to it during religious ceremonies.

The formerly unfavored pigweed is now being condoned and cultivated and even sacrolized by others. What I once perceived as ugly has changed into beauty in my perception since I am a health enthusiast. I am so glad to call you at last my friend, dear pigweed. I highly doubt that I will ever knowingly eat any of that new friend, however.

Allow the Order of the Universe Into Your Life

That there is Order in the Universe is perhaps most apparent to those who long squandered it, or ignored it, and felt the devastating impact. That was the case in my life. How did I ever survive those years when the clutter of Worry and Anger and Fear stalked my life? That I did survive is a tribute to how Order finally works its will through Infinite Wisdom and Infinite Love. It begins at that point when the individual can no longer run away from it. Every path for me was laden with clutter and then came "the blackest of pits." Thank you for the pit that forced me to confront my self-made clutter as barriers to Order and harmony.

The "blackest of pits" in its stark reality is equivalent to a true friend who dares to say, "Look at yourself!" It relates, as well, to the Christian principle that when one is absolutely washed out and ready to give up, then comes surrender time to the Christ principle of God. The Christ principle of God? Yes, that is the Power that gladly moves in and takes over when all personal opposition or ambition gives way.

In effect it is saying, "I can't do it, God. Just take over my total energy." At that point the God energy (Power) becomes operative within the individual as that person becomes as a single drop within the great surge of the powerful ocean. Analogy is the only way it can be described. And even then, one must experience it to understand its impact.

Another way to deal with clutter in your acceptance of it as a barrier to Order in the Universe, is to open wide your closet doors. Take them one at a time. Why not begin with your clothes closet? When we moved from a four-bedroom home into a small condominium unit, we were forced to give away outdated clothing for lack of storage space. That move came, understandably, at a time when I was in the mental set of discarding *things* in my life. Old clothes were a big part of that discard. I called it "sharing with others" rather than discard, because sharing fit in with my desire at the time of serving others in my outreach.

It is a Universal Law that there will be plenty for everyone when the balance of true sharing becomes operative. As I realized this, I was led to share the many clothes I had not worn for years yet continued to hoard for another time when I might want to wear them again. Under the law of sharing, that notion just didn't jibe. And then in an attempt to keep a balance in my closet, I set the rule for myself that a clothing purchase meant an item of clothing to share from my closet. It is always true that there are numerous places where clothing can be used. For the most part I adhere to this rule, but every now and then I forget — or bargain with myself that the give-away will come later. Then I forget.

A case in point is when I recently came home with a new suit. It was my first suit purchase for several years, and this was a particularly treasured one. I smiled with content as I hung it in my closet. It would be just right for an occasion coming up soon on my schedule. Throughout the day, the thought of sharing one of my old suits (giving it away) plagued me. I played games with myself. Oh yes, so I should. But which one? I'd have to think about that for a while. The fact is I was guilty of reneging on the edict I'd kept for so many years. The blatant thought even came to me that I couldn't wear more than one at a time, no matter how much I treasured each of the suits in my closet.

In a matter of days I had a dream in which I was feeling very disagreeable. The frustrating thing was that I was trying to put on layers of my suits. I had two on and was trying to get the third one on over those two when I awoke. It was 2:19 a.m. I bounced out of bed, still angry from the dream and opened my closet door. As I looked inside I mentally shouted, "OK, I'll give one away." By that time I was wide enough awake to see how funny it was. I hurriedly chose a suit, then heard the directive, "a blouse, too." No argument now. Suit and blouse were hung on the bathroom shower rod and I went back to bed, to sleep.

In the morning, the first thing I saw was the chosen suit and blouse. It was a pair I still wore frequently, but at the same time felt good about giving to the house where battered women flee at a low time in their lives.

None of this sharing/give-away is to advocate a program of austerity, although that is a noble mind-set to say the least. This sharing/give-away idea is to keep the clutter from a closet wherever and whenever the individual is ready for it. Such a free choice will bring sure benefits to the one who gives. As well, it will relate to the larger Order of the Universe.

In Summary

In the conclusion of this chapter on Order in the Universe, we acknowledge that the subject has only been touched lightly in its true and deeper meaning and full implications. As a single cell of the mighty Universe, you can best understand the grandiose plan by experimenting with its meaning as you interpret it in your own scheme of life. Clearing out clutter in small ways paves the way to more and broader Order for you. This is the discovery that is inherent in the desire of good intent and the discipline to follow through.

Know that as you are healed through Order and blessed by that healing, you contribute to the healing and blessing of the whole Universe. You become an integral part of the full process which creates Order in the Universe, and each cell of life (such as you are) contributes to that whole.

"In the beginning was the Word," according to the Gospel of St. John. That Word has no less importance today than it had in the beginning. The Word was and is the Power of the Universe. Therefore call forth that Power as in speaking the I am...affirmations, and you create what you earnestly desire for Good. This relates to the Spiritual Law, and those who utilize its Power know its truth from experience. For example, "I am free from the irritations of inconsequentials" becomes a powerful tool in claiming Order. But it cannot help you as rhetoric; not unless you put it into experience will it work its Power through you.

I strongly urge you to use each affirmation in its right place in your plan of life, for every one has been tested many times over in the personal experience of our workshop participants. They have been tested and found effective in change for the Good.

CHAPTER SIX

Finite Mind Experiences Infinite Wisdom

In this seventh decade of my life, one of my most comfortable changes is that I acknowledge the Power of Infinite Wisdom. It is the Force on which my finite mind depends. In all of life, there is a high way and a low way to live. For the remainder of my years I earnestly seek to live within the high way, relying on the collective Mind of God, which Radiant Living knows as the vast storehouse of Infinite Wisdom. It is the Source which in practice operates as Infinite Love. And then Radiance follows.

John Oxenham has written:
> To every man there openeth
> A way, and ways, and a way
> And the high soul climbs the high way,
> And the low soul gropes the low:
> And in between, in the misty flats,
> The rest drift to and fro.
> But to every man there openeth
> A high way and a low,
> And every man decideth
> The way his soul shall go.

It is in experience what we refer to in Radiant Living as making "responsible choices for health and well being."

One of the earliest foundations for this commitment of my later years is the Biblical reference I used so long ago. It was one of the most treasured affirmations of my life: "In all thy ways acknowledge Him, and He shall direct thy paths." Proverbs 3:6 I discovered and remembered that promise, and practiced it, during my painful period of transition. It was the time when I grappled alternately with the "high way" and again giving in to the "low way."

In experience I know it takes an inordinate amount of energy to make decisions on the low road. The same decisions may be made in a completely different mold when you and I discipline our finite mind to allow Infinite Wisdom's way — the high way. For no one can effectively settle a problem on the same level in which it is conceived. Go into the high way of Infinite Wisdom.

Infinite Wisdom is for All

Infinite Wisdom is not designed for a favored few; it is designed for all who allow purity and freedom from barriers. Then there is the long path of trial and error when page after page of the personal journal is filled with the record of desire and discipline and discovery. At first it is the little triumphs, and then in dribbles comes the ultimate. There will be the "long, dark night(s)" followed by spots of enlightenment which with time banish the tears and the pain and the agony.

I have witnessed it all in my own struggles and triumphs. You, too, will have witnessed much of it along your path. I have heard and sensed the "long, dark night(s)" of loved ones and friends and clients. To choose the high way is to feel the burden of many at crucial periods in their lives. I was introduced to the privilege of bearing the burdens of others in a workshop which a beloved leader directed and I was a participant. During an intense meditation session I saw the multitude of people who were hurting; I saw their tears; I felt their intense personal agony. I left the group, temporarily, that I might go apart and weep in expressing my reaction to what I realized as my mission: to be a catalyst in alleviating the hurts of others. The bonus to that is to witness the ultimate joy that leads others into Radiance. For Radiant Living is a group process which builds as millions of tiny lights are drawn together all over the world.

No one of us is more favored than another; we need to remember that, because it is limiting to one's own potential to put a leader on a pedestal and think that level cannot be achieved. The favored are simply those who decide to be all that they can be. Jesus the Christ has been my ultimate mentor, my example, my way. That is because I grew up with Christianity as the rule in my home. Along the way, there were many others who inspired me as they came into my life serendipitously, dressed in a lesser garb than Jesus' shining Radiance. Yet these others were no less sincere in seeking to live the Power Energy of Infinite Wisdom and Infinite Love.

The challenge, moment by moment, is to be in charge of your life with the intent for Good. Learn to 1) sort out; 2) choose priorities; 3) allow endings, and 4) study the alternatives for a fresh start. Let go of Worry. Let go of Anger and Fear. Forego Jealousy. Discover the order in your own surrounding universe so that you may hear "the music of the spheres." As it all begins to hum around you, do not gloat; just give thanks and praise, and continue on the high way.

Normal Experiences Often Seem Like Miracles

There is merit in all of us sharing with others the normal successes we discover. Know that these experiences are not miracles; they are what we may regularly glean from Infinite Wisdom's way when the finite mind listens and trusts.

It is to encourage others that I share some of my own experiences. It is to say that the practice of listening and trusting begins with asking and believing for each of us.

As I write this in Mesa, Arizona, Don and I are on a late winter health trip in a warmer climate than we left behind in Des Moines, Iowa. It is March and we are basking in an outdoor climate of mid-eighties. Imagine, Iowans, needing the air-conditioner in early

March as we hit a high here, unseasonably, of ninety-three. How does it happen that we are here on this impromptu episode in our lives? It was not long-planned and anticipated. It came about because Don needed to sample a warm, dry climate to alleviate his chronic build-up of bronchial asthma. At a time when he expressed the need to bask in some warm dry weather, the opportunity appeared. Don "asked" for the Plan, and we belivingly sought the way. The logistics included my immediate telephone call to my sister Carol in her lovely trailer court in Mesa: "Could you find us a unit to rent for a month?" I believe that answers often come through others as the Power of God directs them to act on our behalf.

The logical way to go in Carol's attempt to find us a trailer brought no yield. Later she thought of another approach, tried that, and an "ifey" possibility developed which she wrote to us in a letter. A day or two later another idea developed in her mind. A single right phone call brought the place we came to in Mesa. Even before her letter reached us with the "ifey" proposal, she called us with a promise of the rental of this trailer. It would be ready for us whenever we arrived.

Even on our first call to Carol, she said, at once, "Come as soon as you can and stay with me until we find a place to rent." Obviously she believed it would develop and Don and I made the pact with Infinite Wisdom that if we were meant to go, the place would appear. So here we are.

When we made that pact, I heard Spirit say, immediately, in the unique way that it comes to me, "You'll go; at the right time it will work out. Get ready." And so I reviewed my commitments in Des Moines and set a timetable for leaving Des Moines on February 18th. That gave me two weeks to wind up my client appointments, set our condo in order, and pack. It gave Don time to plan the route for our motor trip to Mesa. He made our lodging reservations and prepared the car. It became a team effort and in the pre-trip excitement his low-energy state rose to meet the energy necessary to allow us to make the trip in shared driving. Throughout, the sustaining force was the affirmation, "I trust God's Plan for Don's life; I trust God's Plan for my life." All the way, from Saturday at 7:00 a.m., February 18th when we left Des Moines, until the day we arrived in Mesa on schedule, February 21st, we had highways as dry as a desert trail. Our route took us in between periods of snow and sleet and ice, but none of it touched us.

The next episode of finite mind connecting with Infinite Wisdom unfolded when we arrived. Unknown to us, my sister Carol had encountered some recent trauma that became an added blight in her life, already made miserable by some extremely painful dental surgery which started months ago. That dental work kept imposing more and more pain as unusual situations developed. Carol truly needed us for nurturing and for transportation. Carol, who has always been in charge of her life, was able to "lean" on us in her hours of great need. As the baby sister, I was overwhelmed with the flow of love between us. For the first time I felt that I could help her. It was rewarding for me to be able to repay in some small way the mothering she has given me in so many ways, particularly in the death of our mother in 1918 when Carol was but a youngster and I was only a baby.

We also discovered while we were in Mesa that my other sister, Jean, had special needs as well. Her husband had had unexpected surgery and though he was recovering nicely, he was house-bound under strict doctor's orders for two weeks. They could not come to visit us for dinner, so we took the dinner to their house. Carol and Don and I had a wonderful evening of sharing with the two of them.

Later Jean developed a temporary back problem and we were privileged to add our prayers to others for her quick relief. The healing came in short order without any doctor's care.

Don and I have been separated geographically from my sisters for so many years. What joyful therapy it was for all of us to reunite and to share our love, in this our seventh decade of this lifetime.

As we come to survey all of this we are amazed at the precision of God's Plan developing so effortlessly on our part. Spirit moves in marvelous ways, "its wonders to perform." I am urgently reminded that all of it is entirely normal, even as my finite mind foolishly grapples with the logistics.

Another Experience With Infinite Wisdom

In my journal are endless examples of finite mind experiencing Infinite Wisdom. There was our trip through an ice-bound Oklahoma during Christmas time years ago. It was while our daughter, Carol, and husband, John, were living in Dallas, Texas. For days ice storms in Oklahoma and the subzero weather between Des Moines and Oklahoma had kept us from getting to Dallas. On Christmas Day we were still in Des Moines after several planned starts that didn't work out. Early on we had planned that year to go to Dallas early and then travel with them to the very southern tip of Texas for Christmas Day.

Finally, two days after Christmas we were all packed and ready to go in the morning. About 2:30 a.m. I was suddenly awake to hear Spirit's warning, "It's going to be a rough trip." I asked in return, "Shall we postpone again?" The answer, unquivocally, "No, just stay in tune." Basically that meant don't allow the barriers to muddy our directives — barriers of Worry and Fear. At that time, I was completely satisfied with the challenge to *trust*. But as is often the case in my humanness, by morning I awoke to wonder. I said nothing to Don and the trip was on go.

The first day out all went well. No difficulties. On the second day, we awoke in our motel room, just over the border into Oklahoma, to look out on a dreary rainy day. It still didn't seem to be any big problem as we walked to the restaurant for breakfast. We ate hurriedly and started out. Along the way we ran into the warning at a rest stop, "All travel is ill-advised."

Oh well, we had waited so long and we were only a little over four hours from Dallas. Besides I remembered the succinct command to go but "stay in tune." Don's vote was to push-on, as well.

In only a matter of miles we were on ice. At that point we were even wary of turning off; just keep going straight ahead, and pray, seemed to be the best way. That's what we did, joining in a caravan of motor vehicles all going about twenty-five miles an hour. All was well until... Around a corner we came without warning on a pile up of cars. A semi-trailer lay on its side just off the road. And both before and beyond that a number of cars had slid off the road. We joined them. It was not really a ditch, just a level grassy surface, beautifully (or hazardly) coated with ice. The sunshine had come out by then, and the reflection on the ice-covered territory was dazzling to behold. The danger created a strange eerie sight for all its beauty.

All this time, I had the unusual feeling of peace. At once I reached to the back seat and pulled out my wool socks and boots as if to prepare for a long wait. Don got out to communicate with the fraternity of victims. No one was injured; all was quite calm for an accident site involving so many participants. Yes, the tow truck had been called, Don reported. But there might be hours of waiting because the single tow truck in the very small town we'd just passed through, perhaps three miles back, was even now out on a series of other calls.

I just sat there listening and asking of Spirit, "What's next?" But I wasn't getting any answers and I guess that was because Spirit was busily setting things up. Within a half hour time period, several native American Indian men appeared at our window. "This pile up is getting worse," they said. "Is your car OK to go if we can get you back on the road?"

It was indeed, and so they put their strong limbs and bodies to the task of getting some of the cars, like ours, back on track. As we came onto the ice road, our car began to swerve. It was as if Don had no control over the steering. That, of course, is not unusual on ice; but "someone" was certainly in charge of the maneuvers which followed. Suddenly we had crossed the middle-of-the-road line, were turned completely around, and were going back the way we came, safely in the slow-moving traffic in that lane. Don and I were moved to speechless wonder. We exchanged glances, briefly, then concentrated on keeping the car in its lane through his driving and my concentration on "being in tune."

That "miracle" maneuver was the clincher to our earlier conversation while we sat waiting at the icy edge of the road. We had said regretfully and with deep feeling how much smarter it would have been for us to stop at the tiny motel we passed in the little town to which we were headed. We fervently wished in our serious predicament that we had. Yes, we had given a good deal of energy to that thought. But beyond that, we had agreed that even when the tow truck arrived, it could never get us turned around and going back. For it would be working from an extremely icy condition, and even with chains or whatever...no, it couldn't happen. Obviously we weren't aware of God's tow-truck apparatus as the Power collaborated with the human strength of those wonderful Indian men, who had only agreed to get us back on the road in the closest lane.

At a speed of about fifteen miles an hour, the short distance back to that motel we'd earlier passed, seemed endless. Still we knew we'd arrive. When we did, the owner and his Vietnamese wife led us into a spotless motel room. They told us the whole town was without running water because their water main had frozen and burst. But they brought us pitchers of water from the hand pump in their yard. We would have one flush of the toilet for the sixteen hours we were there. For supper we ate the cheese and crackers we'd brought along for travel snacks and opened the home made cookies we'd packed so carefully for Carol and John. When we went to bed we piled our winter coats over the covers to warm our still traumatized bodies. But most of all, we praised and thanked Spirit for all the spectacular care we'd had that day. Don was exhuasted from the tenseness of the drive and fell asleep almost at once. I lay there, wide awake, smiling and smiling and smiling at the wonder of the Power that is God. "All things are possible; only trust." Relating to my finite mind, I felt so insignificant. Relating to my tie with Infinite Mind I felt the Power of God, the energy that created and maintains the Universe.

The next morning we loaded our car and prepared to leave once again on still icy roads, but secure in knowing that the warm sunshine would soon change that. The man in the motel cabin next to us came out, shaking his head. "My wife refuses to even go to breakfast until the ice is gone." We simply smiled and wished them well. We would retrace the way we'd come, which would bring us to a main highway. It would be a little longer, but it would be safer, and we had the whole day ahead of us to get to Dallas by nightfall.

In Summary

My journal is filled with similar cases of Infinite Wisdom in action. And you who read this can no doubt recall cases of your own that match such wonder.

We need only believe that these cases are not spectacular, but that they are normal. For indeed they are normal to all who trust and accept them. That very acceptance will attract more of them in the future.

It seems highly logical that what I have come to accept in these later years was innate wisdom for me at birth. But in all the confusion of my early life, and in the adult sophistication I picked up later, I had to re-learn all that Infinite Wisdom has to offer. It was as though I had to repeat elementary school. What a dunce I was all those years, compared to my present situation of making responsible choices for health and well-being through the flow of Infinite Wisdom and Infinite Love.

CHAPTER SEVEN

Healing, An Adventure in Radiant Living

For a number of years I've had the same poster hanging on my office door. It reads:

> **RADIANT LIVING**
> RESPONSIBLE
> CHOICES
> for
> HEALTH

This poster is one of the visual aids used in our Radiant Living Workshops. During those sessions, the poster stood on the easel, at my right hand, a constant reminder that there were options.

"Responsible choices for health" is a phrase to encourage the subconscious mind to maintain and preside over a healthy body. There is an earlier poster, too. It speaks of "Radiant Body Health ...Becoming the Whole Person."

Both posters have been a reminder to me that I am in charge of my Body, whether in illness or in health. I am through my choices of how I will to use my energy. I can choose to give it away to Anger and Fear. Or Worry, or Jealousy. Or, more wisely, I can recall that "I am not irritated by inconsequentials." In my earlier years, I discovered that when I was ready to let go of the barriers, as we have discussed them in detail in previous chapters, I had a firm foundation for self-healing. This change was one of the educational concepts of Radiant Living Workshops. Barriers impede the healing process.

What do we mean by self-healing? In a sense there is no such thing. The self cannot heal by itself. The self heals in direct ratio to its *awareness* of the true Source, call it Universal Healing Energy, the God Power, Mother Earth, or whatever name according to your orientation. It is the same *awareness* that in Radiant Living calls forth Infinite Wisdom and Infinite Love, the two together manifesting as Radiance. The fact is that the self in recognizing the Healing Power sparks the energy which lights up the genetically programmed healing potential within the electro-chemical processes of the Body. It is the psychological commanding the physiological. Compare it to the electrical circuit within your home; when you manipulate the switch, the electricity flows. The healing Power flows when the mind, in tune with the healing Source, turns on to its acceptance. Or when it provides the clear channel for its flow.

The term self-healing is a potent reminder that you and I are in charge of the healing process within our own Body. Even so, when necessary, we can choose a medical professional as a partner. If we feel we need help for treatment in the form of diagnosis, medication, or even surgery, we wisely turn to that ever available medical partner. But the wisest of medical partners know and affirm in order to bolster the patient's belief, that the patient is in charge of the healing process.

Cells as the Unit of Energy

The cells of the Body as energy units take over the delicate and seemingly miraculous task of healing. And though we do not understand all the intricacies, it just happens, voluntarily. For example, given that the surgeon has done a skillful job of sterilization, cutting, and stitching or clamping, the Body innately knows how to perform the healing. The Mind does not have to voluntarily direct the Body in the step-by-step process. The Body, left with the Mind's clear directive that it wants to heal, goes swiftly and involuntarily about its task. On the other hand, if the Mind worries excessively, or squanders its recuperative power with Anger and Fear, the healing process may be substantively impeded. Many times a low-grade healing is the result of the patient's negative thoughts and unstable emotions. And that very patient is the one whose anger-level is such that he/she is prone to vent that wrath on the surgeon.

Mind you, this is not to take a stand against the patient's right to a skillful scalpel and sterile procedure; but it does emphasize for all of us as patients to be mindful of our expectancy mindset in the optimal process for healing. Let us be as "pure" as humanly possible for us in our resolve to accept complete healing.

The point we are leading into here is that the medical professional is no longer granted the pedestal as high-priest or high-priestess whose word and deed becomes "holier" than the Body being treated. In the self-healing concept, you and I have outlawed the pedestal. That means, of course, we take the responsibility. The patient's Body/Mind is consciously in charge in anticipating the surgery or physical need of healing of any nature. It is except when the Body pain, illness, or malfunctioning temporarily renders the conscious Mind inept. But note thoughtfully, that even then the Mind well steeped in the self-healing regimen automatically calls upon the subconscious to take over, in conjunction with the Source of Power as the healer.

Remember, the Body wants to be well; given the clear channel to healing Power, the Body gets what it wants. I believe that. Do you? If you don't, you must look to re-educating your belief system because it is vital to the self-healing laws. Verifiable research shows that the belief system triggers physiological action within the Body. Accordingly, the belief system enhances the operation of the immune system as the guardian of healing and health; or in negativity (neglect) it programs the breakdown of the immune system. In the latter case, the Body becomes prone to illness, and negligent in the healing process.

Energy, the Agent in Self Healing

In the Body/Mind/Feelings triad, we are talking about the Body as physical energy, the Mind as thought energy, and the Feelings as emotional energy. They interact. They cannot be separated. Each one influences the other two. And the Spiritual being is the circle encompassing the triad of Body/Mind/Feelings. That significant graphic is used on the cover of the companion book by this writer, YOUR RADIANT BODY.

In the first chapter of YOUR RADIANT BODY, "Energy Systems," you may read in detail about the energy of the Body. This knowledge works to encourage your belief system. The opening statement is made:
> Neither health nor illness are locked into your Body; thoughts and emotions create an invisible bridge for change.

On page 6 of this paperback, Albert Einstein's theory of relativity ($E=mc^2$) is cited to endorse the interaction of physical, mental and emotional energies. In explanation of his theory, Dr. Einstein says that matter and energy are not distinct but can be changed into each other. He says, further, that there is an equivalence and interchangeability of energy regardless of its form. And so we apply this to the understanding of the energies of life. No energy is distinct of itself, any more than a single cell as the unit of life is distinct from other cells.

Science tells us that cells communicate through specialized channels built into the membranes which join them. Correct communication between cells is an ongoing procedure in all cells of normal, organized tissue. That communication is crucial to the balance of the Body. Cells need to communicate with significant other cells just as each of us as a conglomerate of cells needs to communicate with significant other people.

Visualize the cell, in its proliferation into some 100 trillion cells of the individual Body, as the microcosm; and visualize the cell in its proliferation into the whole vast Universe, as the macrocosm. Cells relate to cells; they cannot do otherwise. Thus in our awareness of this, we tune into the macrocosm of energy and turn on to profound potential for the flow of healing energy from the Source.

Infinite Wisdom verifies this for us through the mind of Albert Einstein, one of whose contributions to humankind was the theory of relativity. And as an example of how minds as mental energy interact, everyday Infinite Wisdom shows bits of wisdom to others through your mind and mine. Likewise through Infinite Love we serve humanity even as we fulfill our own destiny to be a nurturinng part of the Whole of Life.

The equation of Infinite Love is also explained in YOUR RADIANT BODY, on page 5. The example here comes to us through the mind of Teilhard de Chardin, scientist and theologian, as he wrote in his book, THE PHENOMENON OF MAN:

> Cosmic energy is love, the affinity of being with being. It is the universal property of all life, and embraces all forms of organized matter. Thus the tendency to unite; the attraction of atom to atom, molecule to molecule or cell to cell. *The forces of love drive the fragments of the universe to seek each other so that the world may come into being.* (Italics added.)

In further explanation, we may point out that science sees all things as energy units, while the spiritual approach says humankind is nothing at all if it is not Love. De Chardin as both scientist and theologian, and who, we may add, was surely in tune with Infinite Wisdom, saw significant correlation between the two. In continued explanation regarding his theory on love, there is this quote from YOUR RADIANT BODY:

> The forces of Love drive fragments of the universe together as energy. Love motivates the creation of energy and sustains it as it evolves. Love is uniquely cohesive in that it triggers and develops energy, starting with the affinity of atom for atom (to form cells) in humankind and in the cosmos. Thus all energy interacts with Love. Life is a coalition of scientific and spiritual concepts, a combination of fact and faith.

Experiencing the Cell

The cell as the root of health is the unit of energy. It may be dynamic energy if you so program it. Or it may become low-grade energy as programmed through negative responses to life, which could in time lead to illness.

Every cell has a life of its own; it is unique and fascinating. I never tire of reviewing its electro-chemical processes. One day when I was engaged in intense cellular study, I suddenly wanted the experience of being a single cell. I wanted the experience so I could better understand the dynamics of the individual cell, the better to understand the healing process within the Body politic.

Cleansing my mind of the academics, in deep silence, I slid into the mold of a cell. My first awareness was to the rhythmic, pulsing movement of change. It was a mental and emotional experience, bolstered by intense physical reaction. Here was awareness through the sixth sense. Nutrients, namely oxygen and food and liquid, were being combined in the inherent recipe of life. Waste was being channeled on its course. Purity, my purity as a cell, was paramount.

There were stations within that cell (within me), stations manned by the various organelles, and each with a specific function related to the overall operation. In my first awareness, I was the DNA, scientific name of deoxyribonucleic acid. As the executor of the cell, the DNA was within the nucleus. The nucleus appeared to be the office or headquarters. Here were the genes, in charge of the blueprint for all generations. At once I was awed by the silence of this great operation in its immense implications. That silence melded with the silence of my own inner self. (Pause and time for a couple of very deep breaths.) In that silence I opened up to absorb all the wisdom of the nucleus, but was left without finite words to express it. I knew that I would never be able to put it into words. In that deeper realm, I understood yet there was no translation of it into our finite word-process.

In soundless wonder, I was aware of the ribosomes, engaged in protein building, the main substance of the cell. There was the endoplasmic reticulum, a network of channels used to store and transport proteins to the membrane wall. At the wall, some of the protein particles stood like sentries on a bridge spanning the membrane which enclosed the cellular operation, rendering it like a walled city in its own right.

I saw the golgi, the lysosomes, the mitochondria, the latter marked in my awareness as the powerhouse of the cell, and the first two engaged in the storing and transport of proteins. The mitochondria as the powerhouse was directing cellular respiration and metabolism.

The cell that had become as if one with me was shaped by the microtubules — long, hollow tubes as the outer dimensions of it. Secondarily, the microtubules were a kind of cellular Western Union involved in sending messages back to the nucleus, the head office. I felt breathless, not wanting to intrude or impede the action. Here in the slow-motion of that unusual experience, I saw the grandeur of life — the cell, the magnificant — responsible for the ebb and flow of life. Here was the core of the process of attracting and radiating as we relate to it constantly in Radiant Living. I was Wisdom, and I was Love, receiving so that I could ultimately send forth to others and to all the Universe.

Then it developed that as a single cell I was not alone. Surrounded by like cells, we were a meaningful pattern of life in constant communication with each other. The other cells needed me for life, even as I needed that vast reservoir of life surrounding and supporting me. We were a network, cells sustaining cells. We were a *flow* of Wisdom and Love. It was reciprocal; it was superb. At the time I was no longer a Body; I was a cell. Yet within that intense experience, I knew I was me. That "me" was individual and at the same time a part of Life's Plan of totality. As a person I was a single cell within the vast, yes, Infinite Universe of cells. Like a drop of water, I was significant within the ocean, surrounded by and part of a myriad of significant drops.

At one point my awareness exploded and I was a hologram, a blueprint that carried all the potential of the Universal Life Energy of God. Not just an isolated segment, but a miniscule conglomerate of all the Power, all the Glory. It came to me in music, the music of the spheres: "I am Wisdom, I am Love; aware of God fulfilling Self, a single pattern of All that is." My body and consciousness as a single unit is a cell of the Universe. I am a miniature of the Absolute. At that moment of profound awareness, life was simplistic and complete. No doubts. Yet how quickly that moment passed away. An uncontrolled sigh meant, "Oh, that I could hold onto that treasure forever."

I share this experience because it belongs to you as well as to me. Whoever will listen can share it, for the Infinite Mind reveals whatever the finite mind can fathom. The Infinite Mind reveals it for however long the finite awareness is staid on comprehending, usually a very short time span. For soon the logical left-brain hemisphere dominates the right-brain's innate sense of creative awareness. Even so, when the moment of truth fades from human consciousness that truth remains a fact of life. Truth is a tenuous thread that does not fray just because a single finite mind is no longer aware of it. In my case that moment of truth remains imbedded in my subconscious memory storehouse even after the experience in all its glory has faded. Whenever I recall it, it is scaled to my momentary ability to reconstruct the initial awareness. It is scaled to my momentary belief of that truth.

It lives on for me because I recorded that experience in my journal, recorded it the best I could in terms of my limited finite vocabulary. I do not pretend to fully understand it in retrospect; nevertheless, I know there is truth in the dynamics of what I did record. The truth was embodied in my experience, more than in my description — or analysis — of it.

What I felt has brought me to reflect on my place within the hierarchy of Universal Energy. Scientifically I see that I am atoms, molecules and organelles driven by Love, which gather together as cells. Going up the ladder of the hierarchy of energy, cells form tissues and organs and systems which in Body unison become the self of me. Add Mind and Feelings and self becomes Self with significant spiritual dimensions. Beyond the Self is family, community, nation — all of humankind on our earth world. But that is not the end, either. There is outer space, the solar system, a galaxy of planetary bodies and much, much more. May it be sufficient to say that there is God, knowing that now I am into the realm of the Infinite and mere words cannot say its totality.

Born into a Christian family, I see God embodied in Jesus the Christ and his being is my example. His creed of tolerance also allows me to see the holiness of all religions, regardless of any single religion's Supreme example. I see, for example, that the venerable Buddha is a brother in spirit to Jesus the Christ. We are everyone of us brothers and sisters, One with All. We all have the full potential to be the highest there is. The only limitation any of us knows is created within our own belief system.

Relating to my original experience as a cell, why did I need that awareness? It was crucial to the pattern of healing energy. I needed that awareness because it bridged the gap between me and Thee. It bridged the gap remaining in my finite mind between a single cell and All of Life. I needed that bridge to know that healing energy is an ebb and flow between the finite and Infinite — attracting and radiating. Thus to open my awareness is to open up to the process of constant healing within every cell of my Body. It is an opening to the Source of healing energy. For the theory of change reminds me that if I am not healing, I am deteriorating, since my bodily processes are never static. Healing happens according to my acceptance of self as a hologram of Infinite Power. Healing happens because of "an innate drive in living matter to perfect itself." That is one of the tenets of syntropy as set forth by Dr. Albert Szent-Gyorgyi, renowned world scientist who was one of the most profound thinkers in his field of cellular research. This Nobel Prize winner who told us about Vitamin C, died in October 1986.

Attract and Radiate

When the intensity of that cellular experience wanes, in a moment of secondary awareness, I am once again attuned to the outer illusion of reality. My analytical sense takes over and I say to my Body, "So I'm a cell; tell me what I'm doing." The answer barely waits for the question, as if it were intuiting my doubt. "Creating life; the cell creates and sustains life." Attracting and radiating life, here is a process which permeates all that one is (Body, Mind, and Feelings).

So simple that response, who can question its credibility? I am life. You are life. No need to analyze it. Just pinch that outer garment of cells, called skin, and feel the stab of pain. You and

I are alive, a manifestation of the process of life. It is so simple to conclude that innately the Body wants to live. Life in its unencumbered form is a process of the positive, therefore my Body innately desires to perfect itself (in health). And when health does not prevail, then I must re-search my Mind and Feelings for the barrier I have allowed to interfere.

Metaphysics is being recognized as a science which pinpoints in new and intricate technology the fact that energy fields do exist. The truth is metaphysics reaches beyond the science of physics. The Wisdom that "no man is an island" is proven with scientific certainty through the exploration of these energy fields. The aura as an energy field surrounding the head and torso is observable to highly-sensitive eyes; it definitely interacts with the outer energy field in which it is positioned, according to scientific research. The more sensitive the person radiating that aura, the more vulnerable that person is to whatever energy field vibrations he/she is encountering (attracting). To be in the room, for example, with an angry person is to pick up wild and destructive vibrations. But when the person is not academically aware of energy fields, that person may be temporarily confused by his/her debilitating vulnerability. That person will be confused by the distracting vibrations whether or not he/she is aware of what is happening.

Whenever we are with people we are surrounded by that finely-tuned element of human energy vibrations. It also follows that at times there are volatile energies within the cosmos which affect a particular person, as well. Violent storm disturbances in the atmosphere adversely affect some people who are similarly given to respond with violence. The position of the moon, particularly the full moon, greatly affects the temperament of people. It enhances who they are, whether for love or evil. And beyond these generalities, there are specific planetary configurations that affect each one of us as we lock into the unique energy pattern of our lives at a particular time. These are forces recognized in individual astrology charts. Nevertheless, each of us has the potential to be in control of one's own manifestation.

Change is mental energy and emotional energy before it manifests as physical energy. Metaphysicians have been saying this for years. Now it is being proven in laboratory settings and those who seemed to be on the "far-out" edges of truth can come out of the closet. That does not mean everyone understands this truth even now, but perhaps the burden rests more viably with the disbeliever at this point in time.

A most helpful routine in your own progress would be to keep a Journal of Change. Date each entry and keep a record of significant points in your experience or in your thoughts. Over a period of time you will have data to help you study for and project changes in your future through a comprehensive review of your past. Ask yourself some of these pertinent questions: Where did change work well for me? Where was change erratic happenstance that initiated deterioration? This kind of evaluation is significant because as a spiritual entity, a triad of Body, Mind and Feelings, you can control a self-prescribed pattern of change. Think about your goal; visualize that goal every day and if you are flexible to change the way will appear. Crucial prerequisites include dealing with extreme Fear and Anger, Worry, Jealousy and like barriers.

Experience Your Own Healing

In silence try to initiate for yourself the experience of being a cell. To be aware of a single cell of your Body is to be aware of your base of potential for healing. That healing potential is your innate process. It is not so much to be discovered as it is to be accepted. How can you discover what has always been there, just waiting to be accepted? Again, it relates to your intent — your desire to heal yourself in a moment-by-moment process, both emotionally and physically. Illness is the single, prime factor which seems to awaken the great desire to heal. Yet how unfortunate to wait until the deep need. At that point the low-energy level diminishes your potential. It is also unfortunate in as much as the illness perhaps could have been averted if you had had the will to direct your Body's healing every day, rather than inadvertently allowing a gradual state of deterioration to implode into the waste of Body illness. At any rate, start where you are and allow your thoughts to coax the healing process into action.

My Experience of Healing

To bolster your own understanding of healing potential, I would like to share an experience I had several years ago. I was attending a luncheon in the condominium complex where Don and I live. I had had a traumatic telephone conversation just before I went to the luncheon but did not take the time to center in silence and heal that mental trauma. I didn't take the time because I was already late when I hung up the phone; so off I went. I came into a joyous setting with exhilarated conversation and much laughter — which could at once have been healing. I joined right into the merriment, on the surface, but my subconscious did not let go of the trauma. Within half an hour, I was experiencing dizziness, and only then did I apply relaxation to try to appease the physical. However, physiologically my central nervous system, directed by the brain as the executor, in conjunction with the endocrine glands had seriously upset the rhythm of my Body systems. And in that socially "busy" setting I could not heal my emotional trauma that easily. I could not contact my inner center.

At the onset of dizziness, I excused myself from the gala setting and got as far as the bathroom door when I blacked out. As I fell into the bathroom, I rocked a wicker stand next to the shower stall breaking a number of my hostess' lovely delicate china figures, bumping my head, and landing on my back on the floor. When I came to I was being attended by several of the ladies. I knew where I was, I could clearly see broken china around me, but my Body begged me not to move. My bodily rhythms were completely shattered. At once, I began to program the healing process which is always so effective for me. First of all deep breathing of oxygen.

One of my first thoughts was to wish I were in my bed, for me so synonymous with the healing pattern. In my semi-fuzzy state it seemed to me my bed must be a million miles away. It was that inaccessible. I could not conceive of getting up and walking to the elevator. Nor did I want anyone to help me try. All my physical faculties cried out to the Mind, "Stay right where you are." I'm not sure how long I delayed the luncheon, in itself an agony to me, before someone thought to borrow the wheelchair stored in the complex. Seeing that chair I knew it was my passport to bed, still I closed my eyes again in the agony of somatic disharmony.

With gentle persuasion, the ladies finally coaxed me on my own power into the wheelchair and I was wheeled back to my unit on the floor below. I think I have never been so utterly grateful for my own bed.

What happened from that moment on was a ritual of intense relaxation in which every cell was entreated to resume its normal function. The change was near-instant. Once I was in my bed, alone and in silence, I could concentrate on the healing agenda. I can best explain it by suggesting that my Body is like a mammoth yet finely-tuned physical power structure in which one tiny facet was temporarily out of synchronization. That in turn had sent the total structure into turmoil. In concentrated relaxation, the brain as executor of the central nervous system programmed the inhibiting hormone to replace the flight/fight hormone.

"How Great Thou Art" is the basic theme of my healing. "Thou" comes to mind as the Infinite, yet in healing I remember significantly that the Infinite is within me — as well as surrounding me. I know that my Body is a sensitive electro-chemical entity, sensitive, yet forever responsive. The affirmation I use: "I am a cell, and every cell is a healing station, manifesting life." Not deterioration. I continually affirm that this "remarkable Body" can correct any defect. Again, I assert that your Body has the same potential, according to your awareness.

When my Body is in a state of imbalance I do not consciously think all those details mentioned above, but my subconscious knows those details and automatically proceeds with the treatment.

If the process of healing has never been practiced, or even considered, it is difficult to initiate during the sick or disoriented period. But when you determine through your Journal of Change homework that you are ready to be in charge of your health, you can train yourself in a constant healing treatment day by day. That practice will then become operable at any given crucial moment.

When you do this, amazing results will manifest. And all it takes is one success to make you a believer in your innate potential. I say that from experience. Every added success strengthens my belief. At this point, after long years of self-training in self-healing, I know the truth about my Body and it is, of course, predicated on the many contributing factors, as mentioned before.

I firmly believe that in consciously initiating the process of relaxation and subsequent healing, the mind counters the panic so common to us whenever we feel bodily upset. A look at such panic indicates that we immediately think we must get help. Rightly so, but help from where? We are culturally programmed to think of help as the medical world's prerogative — the doctor, the ambulance, the hospital. They are always the ultimate backup. But the only real help, conversely, comes from within. Ultimately the inner healing mechanism must take over. And so it develops that once we arrive at the hospital, where we know there is all the paraphenalia for help, the panic problem very often abates. It is because that medical territory is like an illusory balm that puts the mind at ease so that it can function clearly and effectively. Very often — except when there is something radically wrong — the imbalance begins to correct itself. It is as if the Mind flashes: "Help is on the way," and then relaxes into its own rehabilitation. When we know and understand this truth of our own healing ability, we can relax into it in bed at home without all the fanfare of going to the hospital. Unless, of course, the artful subconscious seeks all that attention. Once again, however, the going-to-the-hospital elixir is highly significant and necessary when we cannot alleviate the panic on our own, and when we strongly sense that the body imbalance is beyond self-healing without medical help. Each of us must judge our own case.

Many of those kind ladies at the luncheon where I blacked out, asked me later with genuine concern if I had gone to the doctor later for a check up. The suggestions were that I might go in for tests to see what had caused the temporary malfunction in oxygen intake to cause the black-out. I did appreciate their concern. But . . .

No, I did not go to the doctor for tests. No need to. I know my Body, and I know the circumstances at that time. Ever since the years when I constantly ran to the doctor for advice and could not be satisfied, I have programmed my Body to utilize "the doctor within." I know that my Body is sensitive to emotional upset, and I have learned how to bring it back into balance. I simply go with what I know.

This self-healing power did not arise overnight. Some thirty years ago I would have gone immediately to the doctor's office.

Maybe even to the emergency entrance of the hospital. My need then was to rely on someone else's wisdom. Now I can justly rely on the wisdom of my own Body and Mind working together. Since it works, why should I doubt that Wisdom? I am in charge. In Radiant Living I am making "responsible choices for health." Perhaps you are already doing the same thing; if not, you have the potential to do it.

I will not deny that I continue to have, at times, temporary physical upsets, particularly within my very sensitive digestive system. However, I constantly affirm that every upset is temporary because the Body responds in positive manifestation to the positive programming of the Mind and Feelings. I especially have these upsets or imbalances when I have notably abused my Body. Over the Christmas holidays in 1983 I had considerable stress from adverse travel conditions on our way to Dallas to visit our daughter and her husband. I further stressed my Body in Dallas with an excessive intake of holiday sweets, whereas my usual diet includes a minimal amount of sugar. The accumulated stress finally hit me on the way home. I had an extremely sore neck during our motel overnight enroute back to Des Moines. Very simply, I had stored all my stress in my neck, as I frequently do. It was so extremely painful that I began to think about debilitating paralysis. You're right, I was in a panic. When I faced that panic, I knew it was high time for me to get quiet and turn on with healing. First of all, I took a hot shower, with the hot water running luxuriously across my shoulders. The tension release had begun. Then into bed and the all-important technique of overall-relaxation. Very soon my Body began to exalt in the healing flow of bodily warmth. I fell asleep. But alas, that relief was short-lived. I awoke and again felt the stabbing pain when I tried to turn over. Sleep was intermittent, and pain persisted late into the night. Finally I took two bufferin. Rarely do I take any medication with my natural healing treatment, but this pain was more than I could handle without the medication.

A part of my continued panic probably arose because I was away from home and was obsessed with the thought that I must be ready to travel again in the morning. I presume that obsessing thought blocked my Body from full relaxation. Whether I could have accomplished the healing without medication I'll never know.

At any rate, with the medication I was nearly healed by morning and did travel comfortably all the way to our Des Moines home, even though I could still feel slight after affects in the musculature of that extremely stiff neck for two or three days.

In Summary

Each of us is the physician in his/her Body's healing. Hippocrates, the father of modern medicine, has said as much. We need to remember that self-healing is an on-going process, it is a way of life. Its effectiveness originates with the habit of listening to what one's Body is saying in terms of its needs.

Remember that the barriers we have discussed, Worry, Anger and Fear, Jealousy, and the like, are the culprits which victimize the Body in its desire to be well. For the Body is either healing or deteriorating all the time. Moment by moment. Science tells us there is no status quo. As cells regularly die and new ones are born as replacements, the healing automatically takes place. And if we do not confuse the immune system, it operates at a steady pace in combating illness.

At times, for each of us, illness in the form of pain or discomfort to some degree will undoubtedly invade the Body. At that point, just shift into a more intense healing by recalling relaxation through meditation. In a reclining position, be very still and begin at once to praise the Healing Power for taking over. Your Body will respond because it is comfortable with the healing process you have routinely programmed. Continue to affirm: "I am aware that this Body takes care of its every need."

The ultimate healing routine for me is to alternate praise with the mandate, "Relax, relax, relax." The word is said in rhythm with every breath I take, until I fall asleep with "relax," and "praise God" impressed upon my subconscious. Always, I expect to awaken in a healed state, and usually do.

CHAPTER EIGHT

Diet and Nutrition in Self-Healing

Body chemistry is a vital factor in self-healing. That chemistry depends in part on the food we eat in daily diet. The cell we have studied is in its conglomerate arranged into patterns of extraordinary complexity and order. That arrangement is constant, but its parts are subject to continual replacement in the process of metabolism which releases energy necessary for the proper functioning of the Body.

The skin covering that developed to cover you as a fetus, and which covered you at birth, had made a complete cellular change by the time you were seven years old. Throughout your life span, within a seven year period your skin is remade of entirely replaced cells. The fat cells that cushion the skin and keep it aglow are not the same fat cells a year later. Your oldest red blood cells are only four months old, and the entire lining of your digestive tract is renewed every three days.

Change is inherent in the ongoing electro-chemical process of your Body. That change depends on nutritious food for a healthy state. If you decide to junk-food yourself as a way of life, you simply suffer from the cellular suffocation you have imposed on yourself. But given a reasonably substantial diet, your Body gets its way, wanting to be well. The requirements include an assortment of basically sound nutrients in right proportion to each other, and in proportion to the quantity your Body requires for normal weight.

Three Basic Food Nutrients

Carbohydrates, proteins and fats are the three basic constituents of food. They are the ingredients in building, maintaining and healing the Body. Vitamins and minerals, by contrast, are the catalysts prompting the three basic nutrients to interact. Lastly, water or liquid is the remaining component vital to the metabolism and absorption of nutrients and to the excretion of food waste. Your Body can literally survive for weeks without food intake because of its storage reserve, but only for days without the vital component of water. Adequate requirement is six to eight cups a day.

In the companion book, YOUR RADIANT BODY, you will find a detailed explanation of the three basic nutrients, vitamins and water. The more you know about nutrients, the better your health, provided you heed the information.

Food analysis can tell us the nutrient components of each item in our diet. And we find that the Body in a complete chemical analysis shows similar chemical materials. We truly are what we eat. If you weigh 150 pounds, for example, about 90 pounds of that will be water. If that 150 pounds is normal weight for your structure and height, 30 pounds will be fat. The other 30 pounds will be a distribution of protein, carbohydrate, related organic compounds made from them, and the major minerals of your bones: calcium and phosphorus. A mere fraction of a pound is included as vitamins, other minerals and incidentals.

Four Basic Food Categories

In YOUR RADIANT BODY you will also find details on the four basic food categories:
1) Red meats, fish, foul, eggs or cheese
2) Fruits and vegetables
3) Legumes and whole grains as found in cereals and breads
4) Milk products

The ample diet should include at least one item from each food category every day.

One of the factors that encouraged public concern for better nutrition was the report on Dietary Goals for the United States made back in 1977. It was presented by the Senate Select Committee on Nutrition and Human Needs. Whenever the government steps in with a report, or as sometimes with a law, we know the problem societally is a major one. The main thrust of this report was to advise a significant reduction in the consumption of foods high in fat, sugar, and salt. Its warning had a distinctive holistic ring, that We the People rely too heavily on medicine and medical technology, thereby passing the buck in responsibility. The report emphasized the role of nutrition in the nation's two leading causes of death: heart disease and cancer. In the context of responsibility, the report was entirely forthright in its suggestions and warning to us; but you and I must take that responsibility on through our daily dietary intake. Government as a Big Brother does not do the grocery shopping that stocks our shelves, does not prepare our foods, does not in effect spoon the food into our ready mouth.

In our grocery shopping, we need to be ever diligent in reading the labels. Know what ingredients are included in the cereals and breads we buy, for example. The wise shopper includes a wide variety of fruits and vegetables because the nutrients are varied in produce. This does not mean adding quantity, unless you are underweight. It means making substitutions. For example, on various days include carrots, broccoli, cauliflower, beans and so forth, alternately. Potatoes are one of the most nutritious foods we can eat and may wisely be considered a near daily staple. In my childhood home where most of the time we were without meat, or even a variety of vegetables and fruits in the winter months, we always had potatoes. Our basement bin was filled to overflowing from the fall harvest. All five of my siblings and I grew to be healthy adults in part because of our diet of ample potatoes and milk products. All of us are still alive, and in either our seventies or eighties, except my sister, Lorayne. And she soon will be.

Food Quality in Proportionate Quantity

Throughout your years, learn to maintain reasonable weight. Food binging is the sorriest habit you allow yourself — if you do. The sorry part comes when your health breaks and you know that over indulgence contributes to the problem. For one thing, excessive weight puts grave strain on your body joints: ankles, knees, and hips, especially. It also tends to create chemistry imbalance in any number of ways. Another chapter in the sorry story of obesity is the emotional stress of dieting. Dieting probably does not come until a visit to your doctor brings the ultimatum: "Lose 20 pounds and don't expect a balanced body condition until you do." Some physicians in effect say, "Don't take up my time until you're ready to take responsibility for notable weight loss."

If or when you get the weight off, keep it off. Don't ever again allow yourself to overeat. Once you have gone through the agony of losing a great number of pounds, why would you? The up-and-down weight syndrome is extremely hard on the body processes. Figure it this way: The body is confused by your mental behavior which bloats, and then starves. In effect it creates cellular unrest — a kind of anger — which results in notable lack of cellular cooperation for wellness. It seriously jeopardizes the body rhythms.

More than twenty percent over your normal weight classifies you as obese. Please be good to yourself; don't wait for the twenty percent warning. When you hit ten percent over the normal, let mental sirens and bells alert you at once to a stringent diet mindset. Because if you don't, you'll wake up one morning *soon* to discover you've indulged your way into the obese category.

One count says that one in every four adults in America is obese. That adds up to a total of at least thirty-four million obese in this land of plenty. Apart from the obese, further figures show that some sixty-eight million are overweight. In my foreign travels

I have not seen anything like the proportion of overweight people so prevalent in the United States. Obese people are at high risk for serious illness linked to overeating: coronary heart disease, high blood pressure, strokes, and even some types of cancer. Obesity can also cause hypertension and increase the risk of diabetes.

The Report on Nutrition and Health, released by then United States Surgeon General, C. Everett Koop, cited over consumption of fats as a leading cause of disease.

The most staple items of food contributing to high caloric intake which Americans heavily rely on, and which should be modified in intake, are hamburgers, french fries, and ice cream. Are they your favorites? Try to adapt your menu to include more fruits and vegetables and whole grain breads. Don't be ordered around by that saucy palate of yours which daily screams to appease its taste buds. Who's in charge, anyway? Think it through long range and decide whether you want to live a productive and comfortable life. The other path has brambles of illness at endless spots along its miserable course. Making "responsible choices for health" may be one of the changes sorely needed in your wellness agenda.

Researched studies in gerontology urgently indicate that it is possible to hold back the aging processes by eating less food. Studies show, for example, that spiders, fruit flies, silkworms, caterpillars, guppies, mice and rats all live significantly longer with dietary restrictions. I don't know that I want to be compared with any of the above, but it does seem to indicate a trend. At the least, I like to compare it with the significant factor we've already discussed of not overeating as an element of all-around health — for every day we continue to age, whether in the forties or beyond.

Corporate America Endorsing Nutrition

It is a mounting trend for corporate America to include cafeteria facilities for their employees. In that cafeteria, they make an all out effort to serve nutritious meals. In Des Moines, for example, American Republic Insurance and Principal Financial Group are two of the companies that provide a nutritional menu with good options. In many cases, to the credit of the employees, it is they who ask for it. And to the credit of the employer, their response has been cooperative. Some are even supplementing their nutritionally sound service with classes which educate on the subject of nutrition. The classes are offered during the noon hour by granting attendees an extra fifteen minutes.

An additional bonus factor is that many employees carry the nutritional knowledge home to their own family kitchens. Good nutrition fosters weight loss as well. Long range, employers know that nutritious food in their cafeteria equates with less illness benefits and lost-time hours.

In Summary

It would seem that Americans are collectively listening to improved nutrition. Let's hope this continues to spread, for as a nation we sorely need to help ourselves to an improved overall health picture. We truly cannot afford to be sick for health care costs continue to mount. The catastrophic health care picture has developed in some part through negligence on the part of We the People. We are all being held accountable to shape up to making "responsible choices for health." Let's you and I do our part.

CHAPTER NINE

Exercise in Self-Healing

Exercise is not necessarily the fast lane to health, but it is one of the tracks. It is at the least a subsidiary insurance policy for those who engage in exercise wisely and on a daily basis. I can vouch for this from years of study and experience.

As a part of my advocacy of self-healing, I see self-initiative and daily discipline in the sports area as crucial. There are so many bonus features to body maintenance. I'm relating, of course, not to spectator sports but to active participation through a serious commitment to one's own agenda. And I commend exercising to your own drumbeat above that of group dependence. You don't need to pay dues to a health center and try to adjust to their schedule. It does have some merit, and if that is your way, right on. But your own agenda can be just as effective and less costly.

One of the most frequently used excuses I hear for not exercising — zero-exercise agenda — is that "I don't have time." As long as you claim that problem you will continue zero-exercise. You will continue to cheat your Body of the many benefits to accrue from making time.

We must learn to honor the fact that the Body structure is built for physical activity. It thrives on a wise program of exercising unless you have a unique physical disability.

When we come to the structuring of fitness we start with the cells that form the muscles of the Body. The musculature throughout the Body is extensive, and includes the heart or cardiac muscle. Exercise on a daily basis helps to maintain these muscles in flexible fitness. It keeps the individual cell alert.

Hypokinetic Disease

Our culture today has adopted the mold of a busy stressful format. "No time to exercise" is the epitome of this format, although in fairness many do make time. They do because close range they feel better after a workout. They also exercise because they are serious in wanting to continue the productivity of a busy life.

What do we mean by hypokinetic disease? "Hypo" means too little, and "kinetic" means activity or energy. "Too little activity" is what we're talking about. What this leads to includes such examples as heart disease, lowback pain, diabetes, and obesity. What we strive for to counter these problems is physical fitness. We need to keep the muscles flexible through movement and to encourage the Body in its potential to function well at all times. This has to do with balance and coordination. Body rhythm is a flow of movement which is only possible when the musculature is lucid, meaning here that it has full use of all its potential as the mind directs it.

The term hypokinetic disease was coined in the early 1960s. That period marked a new era when medicine had effectively eliminated most infectious diseases, so that the epidemics that had devastated us for years were almost entirely gone. Now we had the crossover into a society being stalked by a different disease, the degenerative, stress-related, one characterized by the sedentary living. It was as if we had to have some kind of health problem. And so we attracted the long term muscle-clutch with its attending pain. We did it in ignorance. A great many are paying the price these many years later with the chronic and excruciating pain that sometimes abates but never really leaves the muscles in normal flexibility.

The hypokinetic disease pattern is a bleak one, one that has been enlarged to the statistic that lowback pain is today number one in treatment clinics. The good news is that if you have not succumbed to the muscle clutching syndrome, there awaits you the wisdom that a pound of prevention (through daily exercise) far surpasses the pound of cure after the onset of pain. It surpasses because by the time the cure is necessary, pain has often been locked in for too long a time to be easily alleviated. And in the meantime, the agony could be excruciating. In contrast, exercise keeps the muscles flexible.

Years ago when I was locked into a public relations career in a rigid office position of high stress, I read about the health prognoses of stressed muscles and their impact on lowback pain. I was just beginning to experience that pain at the time. It alerted me to take frequent breaks from my desk — just to walk about on a short errand, and to raise my arms and to rotate my head as I walked. I tried to move into a hallway where no one would see me. But as you may guess, I was "caught" more than once in my seemingly wild gyrations. In time I was bombarded with questions, and what developed was an office full of people who also had adopted strange gyrations as a safe guard against the hypokinetic syndrome. Or even better news, the strange gyrations became a practice designed to alleviate the lowback pain already being endured by many in that office.

What Is Muscle?

When we understand the muscle it is easier to handle our treatment of it. It is a bundle of long slender cells, resembling fibers, that have the power to contract. They also have elasticity and are capable of being stretched and of performing reflex actions. All of this is made possible by the motor and sensory nerves operating through the brain and spinal cord. The muscle cell ranges in length from a few hundred thousandths of an inch to several inches. It also varies in shape, and in color from white to deep red.

Each muscle fiber receives its own nerve impulses and each has its own fuel supply of glycogen. Some muscles, such as the heart, also use free fatty acids as fuel. Triggered by an intricate signal from the brain/mind, the muscle fiber changes chemical energy into mechanical energy. The result is muscle contraction which creates movement. When a muscle has depleted its supply of glycogen and other substances, and accumulated too much lactic acid, it loses its flexibility. At that point it suffers from muscle fatigue which is the state we may aptly call muscle clutch. Basically it means that the muscle cannot relax. In that stiffened inflexible state long term, the musculature shortens and locks into a painful clutch.

The message for muscle contraction comes from the brain as it collaborates with the spinal cord, both of which are components of the central nervous system. It is a process of signals sent to the spinal cord from what is known as the motor area of the celebral cortex in the brain. These signals may affect the gross muscular adjustments used in manual labor or the tiny adjustments such as in finger movement.

Muscles are fascinating cellular entities. They deserve our respect. They deserve our cooperation in exercising them carefully so they do not become locked into the clutching form we subject them to in daily combat under stress. About once a year, at least, it seems we should have a national "I love my muscles" day. A daily Body hug might be the reminder to say to our loved ones, "Relax, muscles; this hug's for you." Unclutching muscles in America today has a major role; let's face up to the painful need in this stressful society.

The Treatment of Clutching Muscles

The manifestation of clutching muscles from long term stress is varied, and until the process is understood it may seem to be an unrelated response. Some common examples other than those already mentioned include migraine and stress headaches, foot problems, stiff joints, insomnia, and eye problems such as burning, twitching, itching, and swelling. It is not always apparent to the victim that the stress in his/her life is the presenting factor. And even when stress is accepted as the culprit, opposed to that factor of knowing is not knowing how to alleviate the pattern.

In answer to the urgent need for treatment of muscle pain today, some very sophisticated and meticulously designed exercise and movement techniques have evolved. These techniques administered by well trained clinicians most agree are safer long range than the risk of surgery which is never guaranteed. We may call this new breed of clinicians somatologists in keeping with their knowledge of the Body or soma. They work from a thorough knowledge of anatomy, physiology, and kinesiology, dealing with the basics of balance and postural alignment. The effectiveness for the stressed person comes with the ability of the somatologist to understand the muscular patterning that has developed in the individual Body, leaving the victim in such pain. The somotologist applies hands-on to correct the faulty, deepset muscular aberrations. When simpler techniques have failed to produce results, this knowledgeable approach has the potential to accomplish an effective breakthrough.

Beyond what the trainer can potentially accomplish with the stressed person, actual change over a period of time depends on the stressed person's commitment to bodily improvement and change through self-discipline. Once again we are reminding the victim in pain that the actual healing process is inherent in him/her and that his/her reaction to the treatment is beyond what the trainer can do.

Some of the terms being applied collectively to these unique exercise regimens include Functional Integration (of deepset muscles), Awareness Through Movement, Structural Integration, and Eutony. The common term at square one might well be somatosensory, or awareness of one's own body functions; this would be the training which makes it possible for one to detect when and where the muscles are settling into a pattern of inflexibility, or clutching. These deeply applied exercise patterns and the attending awareness gradually educate the individual to feel the tightness before the problems begin. A simple example would be the set of tenseness countless people carry in neck and shoulder muscles, the tenseness which may well move down into the lowback pain in time.

What the somatologist is dealing with are cases in which a state of mental anxiety has endured long term, becoming chronic, with the inevitable result of extensive malfunctioning in some strategic area of the body. In that altered body-set, deterioration is rife at the cellular level, and that speaks to the depth of the renewal. The easy flow of cellular communication is restricted, tense muscles are clutching, joints lose their range-of-motion and become rigid, and/or shallow breathing sets in because as another faulty feature, the diaphragm muscle in the midriff becomes restricted. With faulty breathing, the oxygen supply to the Body diminishes and the muscles suffer yet another inadequacy. The list of problems proliferates even as each one becomes ever more intense. Muscles in general are said to cramp and others consequently droop into flabby uselessness. The hurt creates poor body habits with every movement a struggle. What happens when it hurts to move? The Body steels itself against that hurt, with its victim moving less and less, making a bad situation even worse. What a dilemma.

All of this educates us to the wisdom of exercise as preventive treatment before discomfort and pain are locked in. But it also alerts us that once in pain, there is help available through extended treatment from professionals who understand the body's musculature. Yet the battle to regain comfort is often a long one.

The factors discussed in previous chapters relating to barriers such as Worry, Anger and Fear, apply in the long run to muscle clutching as well. And the physical movement of exercise on a regular basis also helps to alleviate the psychological mind stress, even as it physiologically alters the muscle tension into flexibility.

The Character of Fitness

Fitness is the potential you have to be comfortable physically and to be productive as long as you live. The emphasis is not on quantity of years, but, rather, quality of life. Some will smile and think that definition quite nebulous. On the contrary, it is entirely straightforward in that to be productive is uniquely personal and so each life develops according to priorities. You may enjoy the work world and maintain your career through the seventy year old mark now enacted into law. Others may declare their employment retirement early so that they may "get on with living as they choose." If the Body has been maintained in fitness, that comfort will spawn years of joy by whatever pattern is applicable. Fitness does not mean dollars to join a health club. It does not mean expensive equipment with which to work in developing muscles. More simply, it means determination and the will to exercise, again, according to your own plan.

The most popular sports involvement for fitness currently is walking, swimming, bicycling, simple calisthenics and jogging or running. No need to belong to a health center to participate in any of the above. Nor do any of them require a specific skill. Provided your health is not noticeably faulty, just start in and do any one of them, or several different ones, at your own sensible pace. Be moderate in the time and speed you give to whatever sport you choose. Other factors to consider in determining a health agenda are your age and your Body's potential based on genetics.

The one expense that could pay good dividends is the purchase of a pair of special walking or jogging shoes. Features included in such a shoe are a high back to support the achilles tendon, a wide, cushioned, and elevated heal, good arch support, and adequate room for the toes. The exterior of the heel should be rounded and the exterior sole should be flexible with a rippled or dimpled tread. The average supportive walking shoe can cost you in the fifty dollar range, but in foot, leg and joint protection the financial cost will be well spent. Furthermore, if you walk every day, you will need to replace the shoe every six to nine months. Replacement depends on how you wear down the supportive parts of your shoe. It is wise to use a shoehorn to slip your foot into the shoe so that you do not break down the high back of the shoe.

In terms of foot and leg comfort, so vital to overall wellness, shoes are my most expensive item of clothing today. I treat my feet like royalty. Long ago I stopped wearing my high spike heels for dress shoes. I live comfortably in the lower height that have width for good support. I came to this conclusion after "listening" to a knee joint complain every time I indulged my vanity with shoes that looked so much more "sexy." My knee joint never hurt until the next day or maybe even two days later. It took me a long time to trace down the cause. I share this because I hear many women talking about knee discomfort. I suggest they check out their shoe closet.

Benefits of Moderate Exercise

What are some specific benefits of daily moderate exercise? Let's start with the heart, so vital to life and so misused today. Essentially the heart is a muscle pump, and exercise can make it more efficient. Exercise gives the heart the potential to meet the demands of strenuous activity with fewer beats because it can pump out more blood with each contraction. In fitness you are better able to extract oxygen from circulating blood, reducing the demands on the heart. Another important factor the lay person does not usually know is that with the healthy heart there is less buildup of fatigue inducing lactic acid, the waste product of muscle activity.

Recently at an airport, I was extremely glad I had a good heart or perhaps I would not be here to write this chapter on fitness. I came into O'Hare, Chicago, late for my connection to Des Moines. Just as I entered the terminal the last call was blaring out for my connecting flight, "All passengers should now be on board," according to the loud speaker. I was probably three blocks distance on the concourse from that plane. I ran. I walked. I ran. My carry on bag got heavier and heavier. I was breathless. Barring a dead Body, there was no way I was going to stay in Chicago overnight, and it was evening then. Finally I began to shout to the redcap I could see down the line in that nearly deserted area: "Hold the plane, I'm coming." At that point, the redcap called out to a wheelchair attendant, very near me, "Give that lady a ride." I hadn't even seen the wheelchair; it was as if it fell from "above."

Coming up behind me, he literally swept me into his chair, while I nearly lost my flight bag in his generosity. As he whisked me the remaining distance to the gate, the attendant there said, amiably, "No problem, lady; we knew you were coming, that your plane had just landed." I ran onto the plane and the door clamped shut behind me. Some few of the passengers even cheered this white-haired, breathless lady, with my carry-on bag that seemed to weigh a ton in that mad race. Even granted waiting for our turn in the flight pattern to take off, we were well into the sky before my heart settled down. Hurray for daily walking and swimming!

Regular exercise helps to maintain the pumping of blood which skews blood-fat-levels in maintaining cleaner arteries. It reduces triglyceride and even changes total cholesterol levels. It tends to increase the good-guy HDL cholesterol. HDL is believed to be the "scrubber" action that cleans arteries of the LDL cholesterol which tends to cling to arterial walls. Conversely, exercise tends to reduce the LDL level.

As a big plus, moderate daily exercise is a natural tranquilizer, and works concurrently as an anti-depressant according to need. The physiology of it is that exercise encourages the release of the brain hormone, beta endorphin. This is the Body drug that acts much like morphine. When you come home from a walk feeling good physically and confident psychologically, give that internally released endorphin the credit.

Moderate exercise with careful attention to warm-up and cool-down, will prove an aid in keeping pain free mobile joints. It very likely wards off the painful and crippling effects of arthritis, if the exercise starts early enough before it gets deep seated. Some ten years ago I had considerable arthritis. It was the kind that moved from a thumb joint, for example, to an elbow, to a knee. It would come and go, but when it came it stayed long enough for me to remember the pain of it. A year or two into my daily exercise agenda of walking and swimming, I realized the arthritis had left me entirely. I have not had it since.

Diabetes may be improved through exercise, also. Exercise increases the body's sensitivity to insulin. As the pancreas is stimulated in moderate exercise, it automatically steps up the release of insulin which clears excess sugar from the blood. For the seventy-five percent of adult-onset diabetics who are overweight, exercise helps to reduce Body fat, and is a safeguard to insulin flow.

Weight-bearing exercise, such as in walking or running as opposed to swimming, stimulates the calcium content of bones which is so vital in preventing osteoporosis. The loss of bone mass in osteoporosis increases the potential for debilitating fractures as women reach their later years.

As a complement to walking or running, however, swimming as a regular exercise is invaluable. It increases generalized muscle tone and flexibility by unlocking clutched muscles. As the water strokes the body muscles it tends to relieve tension. And in the sports world, swimming has the least number of injuries. Those who are afflicted with painful arthritis find swimming to be a comforting exercise for water tends to suspend the Body so that gravity and anti-gravity forces are practically eliminated. Swimming uses many Body muscles, but mainly those of the upper body, as opposed to the muscles of the lower Body used in walking. Hence utilizing both walking and swimming provides a substantial exercise format.

A Reminder on Smoking

There is one more reminder that you may or may not need. The subject is smoking. If you do, please don't. Please, please, be good to yourself. Let exercise alleviate the strain of your Stop-Smoking celebration.

Smoking is the most devastating of all non-health patterns. The use of tobacco ravishes the electro-chemical processes of the Body.

The American Heart Association and the American Lung Association offer the following benefits to those who stop smoking:

1) Within 20 minutes of the last cigarette blood pressure drops to normal, pulse rate drops to normal, Body temperature of hands and feet increases to normal.

2) After 8 hours, carbon monoxide level in blood drops to normal and oxygen level in blood increases to normal.

3) After 24 hours, chance of heart attack decreases.

4) After 48 hours, nerve endings start regrowing and ability to smell and to taste things sharpens.

5) After 72 hours, bronchial tubes relax, making breathing easier and lung capacity increases.

6) After 2 weeks to 3 months, circulation improves, walking becomes easier, and lung function increases up to 30 percent.

7) After 1 to 9 months, coughing, sinus congestion, fatigue,

and shortness of breath decrease; cilia regrow in lungs, increasing ability to handle mucus, clean the lungs and reduce infection; Body's overall energy level increases.

8) After 5 years, lung cancer death rates for average smoker (one pack a day) decreases from 137 per 100,000 people to 72 per 100,000 (after 10 years, rate drops to 12 deaths per 100,000 — or almost the rate of nonsmokers.)

9) After 10 years, precancerous cells are replaced; other cancers — such as those of the mouth, larynx, esophagus, bladder, kidney, and pancreas — decrease.

There are 30 chemicals in tobacco smoke that cause cancer.

It is highly encouraging to report that according to a Louis Harris poll, only 26 percent of Americans were smoking in 1989, the lowest number to that date.

Less encouraging, however is the report that more people than ever are overweight — 64 percent compared to the previous 60 percent — as of 1989 count. We have managed to maintain our status as the fattest nation on earth, according to a recent Prevention Index report.

In Summary

The bottom line in exercise is stimulation of the respiratory system — the breathing apparatus. When you are locked into a stressful office environment and feeling overwhelmed with it, help yourself to more breath even when you cannot get away on a healthful break. Sit quietly at your desk and deep breathe way down to your lower torso. Inhale and exhale in slow rhythmic measures. Do it perhaps four times; more than that and you may wind up light headed from excess oxygen. Then for a few brief moments, visualize yourself sitting in a lovely flowering garden. "Relax, relax, relax," Just say it non-verbally. Flex your fingers, rotate your ankles, massage your shoulders. And don't look around you to see who's watching!

Feel good? Go back to work at a somewhat slower pace. You'll get more done, long range, than in the hurry, hurry, hurry syndrome.

Only you can take care of you. Only you, likewise, can suffer the pain of building up tight, inflexible muscles if you bring the dire consequences upon yourself through neglect. Celebrate today as an "I love my muscles" observance.

CHAPTER TEN

Radiant Living Adapts To Disease or Disability That Will Not Let Go

Radiant Living is the study and practice of *preventing* disease and disability.

Radiant Living is also the study and practice of *adapting* to disease and/or disability when it claims the body and will not let go.

Radiant Living chooses complete and permanent healing, but sometimes that healing is delayed until another lifetime. The reason for that delay is often unclear to the one that suffers. Some question, will this battered-body pattern come again with the birth of a new lifetime?

It is my belief that a Radiant Spirit, evolving from the practice of *serenity* in this lifetime, will abandon in death's transition the battered-body pattern, assuring itself of wholeness in the succeeding lifetime.

Serenity. It is a magnificent test of will-power to accept serenity beyond the denial and anger and fear that stalks the mind housed in constant physical pain. To accept serenity is also to understand how inner peace is possible.

Trust is the discipline. Absolute trust that never wavers, except perhaps, temporarily, in short time spans.

In those short time spans, it helps to come back repeatedly to the affirmation, "I trust complete and permanent healing." This is always a valid affirmation, recalling that the healing, nevertheless, may not appear until Spirit leaves the physical body to cremation or the grave.

High level trust further believes that persistent pain can be endured. It can be endured, yet in that endurance the mind is not condoning pain as a "welcome visitor." There is a fine line between endurance and condoning, and the mind must ever be alert to it. Yet the mind adapts, day by day, to what it cannot change — for that, too, is part of healthful living.

Meanwhile, the mind must patiently encourage the body with the valid affirmation: "Pain, go away." Or as an alternative, affirm, "Pain, I do not accept you." This identifies pain as an adversary which makes it possible to confront. You are saying in effect, "Pain, you're here but not invited." Like any unwelcome visitor to which you would adapt, you reserve the thought that pain will go away eventually.

For all the adapting to pain, one continually carries in the subconscious the trust in Healing Energy. That trust generates Healing Energy as a power — Healing Power. It is that power which activates, even in short spurts, as the conscious mind struggles to adapt.

Healing Energy as Power

The burning question that springs eternal in the mind of the pain victim, and who repeatedly asks for explanation, is this: What is Healing Energy?

The answer is as simple as the Story of Creation, as simple and yet profound. All things created at God's direction, or at the discretion of Universal Spirit — whatever your orientation — sprang from the first splurge which is an Energy Field. A vast Energy Field, unfathomable to human comprehension, was that from which all manner of forms emerged.

It is a marriage of science and religion which verifies that initial Energy Field. Extraordinary scientists such as Teilhard de Chardin and Albert Einstein were also theologians in sensing the spiritual. Dr. de Chardin in THE PHENOMENON OF MAN told us that Love is the force which activates that vast energy into the forms we accept as God's Creation. Dr. Einstein told us that all energy is interchangeable, interacting, never disappearing, but only changing form.

So in the beginning was the Word, and the Word was with God as God created forms one by one from the vast Energy Field. A simple household analogy is the pan of dough from which the baker creates forms such as rolls or loaves of bread.

The forms of Creation became great galaxies of stars and planets which we cannot fully comprehend because our vision of them is so limited. Men and women who journey space come back in great awe from having viewed the planet earth in a new and phenomenal sense never before experienced.

We are more familiar with other forms of Creation if we choose to take a closer look: the awe of a morning blush of light coming out of the darkness of night — dawn, as we call it. It is the action of Energy, the sun's energy. Or witness the unfolding of a flower that presents its blossoms. We are a part of these Energy forms because all of Creation is interchangeable Energy.

To look further, we see plant life on land and in the vast ocean depths, as modern technology through exquisite photography brings us underwater viewing; lower animal life, including birds and insects; greater animal life, such as you and I, as examples that portray the Wisdom and Love of Infinite Mind. All of these forms from the selectivity of God's direction, utilize the same initial form of energy as the great cosmos of stars and planets. Hence we see the interaction of the microcosm and the macrocosm.

Within that vast Energy Field of Creation is the Healing Energy that proliferates life, ever renewing in its constant cycle. Man and woman seldom acknowledge this, or else why would you and I doubt that Healing Energy is always available? The answer is simple: it is our petty, our pea-size, *awareness*. We are so beset by life's confusion and turmoil that we neglect the factor of trust, which would bring to us the full picture of our healing potential.

When we drop all doubt for a momentary period of trust within the pattern of serenity, then we can "see and feel" Healing Energy. At that point, we enact Healing Energy in the physiological processes of our physical body. If we can hold that trust long enough, we are healed, completely and permanently. But we are entirely human, remember, in our ability to comprehend. And so we only rarely allow what we are still calling "miracle healing."

Trust is a discipline. Come back to it repeatedly in the affirmation: "I am completely and permanently healed."

Pain-Relief Through Endorphins and Enkephalins

Simultaneously, as we trust Healing Energy, we need also to activate the body's own pain-relief process. This pain-relief process is characterized by opiate-like substances called endorphins and enkephalins. They are produced in the brain and spinal cord. They are produced most effectively at the discretion of positive thoughts and stable emotions. Pain-panic reduces their potential to function freely. Here we're talking about mental panic induced by body pain.

Endorphins and enkephalins, classified as peptides in the scientific community, are substances which lock into specific receptors at the sites of their production in the brain and spinal column. They reduce the experience of pain and in part help the organism to feel a sense of serenity. Endorphins and enkephalins have also been found in the intestines and adrenals.

These natural opiate-like substances tend to anesthetize the physical body against responding, or over-reacting, too directly and forcefully to negative, cognitive stimuli found within the painful physical body or to a distressing stimulus found in the outer environment of turmoil.

What Is Pain?

Pain is a warning which indicates the body is in imbalance. The secretion of endorphins is the body's mechanism to soft-pedal that pain alarm. For some the pain-relief process of stimulating endorphins and enkephalins is more responsive than in others. This is to say that pain and its threshold is highly individualistic. Perhaps this has to do with whether the mind clings to anger and fear, or conversely, whether it has a history of serenity. It could also work in reverse where the ample flow of endorphins makes the serenity level easier to achieve. At any rate, when the pain victim can tune into meditative relaxation, this assists the pain-relief process of endorphins to activate.

The activation of endorphins causes a vague reaction that is different according to situations. For example, when you have a fever the result may not be actual pain, but, rather, a feeling of sluggishness and depression in varying degrees. It usually prompts you to seek bed rest, which is the wise prescription.

During a fever test induced into a study of sheep, researchers found that endorphins pour from the animal's pain-relief process in the brain and spinal column. At the height of the fever, blood endorphin levels rose seventeen times higher than before, and concentration in the spinal fluid was ten times greater. When the animals received doses of noloxone, a medicine that blocks the action of narcotics in the body, their secretions shot up even higher. It appeared that the body tried all the harder to come to the aid of its physical condition. These tests were made by researchers at Harvard Medical School, as reported by the news media in August, 1982.

Endorphins and enkephalins are classified scientifically as peptides, an amino acid substance, a member of the body's hormone secretions. The blood carries them to significant locations of receptor sites as they activate the pain-relief process.

What we see is that an imbalance within the body creates pain; yet we come equipped with a body mechanism which also controls pain. That potential to control pain is activated according to our *awareness.* We must awaken to its power.

It is like holding in a tight fist a million-dollar jackpot. Until you spend it to live more fully, the power is useless. But like the million-dollar jackpot, use the pain-relief process wisely.

Accept the endorphins and enkephalins as a part of your sanctity of life, activating them within a mileau of relaxation and inner peace known as serenity. Establish that serenity as a way of life and within the ensuing body harmony your physical pain will diminish — perhaps disappear. At the least, your pain will become tenable as you *adapt* to it, even if you must still use a minimum of pharmaceutical analgesics to help out.

In the birthing process, we become heirs to Healing Energy and the Pain-Relief process. No other inheritance, monetary or otherwise, can match that pair.

Respect your body and be *aware* of its full potential. Don't short-change yourself. Feel good about who you are. Talk to your body and "listen" to its response. *Your body wants to be well.*

Recall every day that you are an integral form created within the Energy Field of Creation. Your energy is a cell of life.

Massage the area where pain is rampant. Think of your hands as giving your body a love treatment for healing.

As you massage, smile and hum, as if you were a beautiful cat, purring.

All of these measures encourage relaxation, along with the affirmation, "I am accepting my responsibility for Health and Healing."

Chinese Qi Gong, Acupuncture and Moxibustion In Experience

In late September and early October of 1988, I was in China (Beijing, Shanghai, and Guangzhou) for a brief study of their traditional healing techniques. Before I went I read and studied a great amount of material recommended by our tour guide. And since I returned, I've never stopped reading. It is all so fascinating.

Our first stop on this study tour was in Beijing at the Qi Gong Research Department at Xi Yuan Hospital. Dr. Lu Chang, director of the Research Department, and Doreen O'Sullivan, an American student studying Qi Gong and Acupuncture, met with us to explain in brief what they were doing with their patients.

One of those we observed had an ulcer in his esophagus; another had hematoma of the brain. There were patients with eye disorders, some who complained of seriously disruptive sleep patterns, and others with respiratory problems such as asthma, bronchitis and emphysema. There was a broad range of disorders and for the most part, all had been previously treated with Western type medication that had produced little or no response.

A thirty-one year old patient had been diagnosed some six years ago with rheumatoid arthritis. Western medicine had not brought any improvement. Here in the Qi Gong Research Department at Xi Yuan Hospital there was strong evidence of marked improvement after only a six-week treatment.

We were told that dietary changes were an important part of the Qi Gong treatment. Dr. Lu Chang emphasized that for best results, all hot and spicy condiments were eliminated. He explained, as well, that nutritional quality was important, and in the right quantity. Over eating stresses the body and that is especially relative when the body energy is being utilized in healing. Another factor that was definitely significant was the mental outlook. Early on, in my own appraisal, I saw Qi Gong's many similarities to our holistic approach in the United States.

The doctors' rounds in this Center were unusual by American standards. The Qi Gong healing method was geared to daily stimulation of the body's vital force — the Qi. These doctors took the responsibility of enhancing the patient's awareness of the Qi. The verbal exchange of "How are you feeling today?" was a short interlude of question and answer. Following that the Qi Gong doctor continued with the treatment in which he or she seemed almost in a trance. He or she would strike a stance which reminded me of one of the martial arts, Tai Chi.

In a simple description, the doctor's arms were extended, the hands rhythmically undulated, as the body swayed, always, in rhythmic motion. The doctor shifted weight from foot to foot.

What was happening? In most cases, acupuncture needles protruded at some point from the patient's body, and the brief healing round was directed to stimulating the body at that particular energy point of the meridian. The doctor never physically touched the patient, but it was obvious to me in my sensitive monitoring of the procedure that the Qi Gong doctor "touched" the patient's Qi in a very realistic way. When I was close to the healing demonstration, I could feel the energy flow. The doctor was testing the patient's energy flow to detect improvement, and he was also reportedly sending out energy vibrations that enhanced the patient's natural healing process.

These brief "hands-on" sessions by the doctor were complemented by a cooperative patient who entered into the exchange with readied *awareness,* anticipating the Qi Gong treatment. As nearly as they were physically able to participate, according to the level of illness, the patient also entered into additional prolonged periods of daily exercise which enhanced their *awareness* and therefore their receptivity of energy stimulation. Healing in this Research Department was more than passive bed rest. With the highest motive, they were *adapting.*

Later it all came together for me far more clearly as I watched a concentration of the Chinese in their daily exercises outside, in the parks and boulevards. On my early morning walks, in each of the Chinese cities we visited, I saw great numbers of Chinese participating in the various disciplines of martial arts and the related Qi Gong exercises. Their exercising was far more common than the few joggers and walkers I've encountered on my daily early morning walks in Des Moines, Iowa. The Chinese turn out from their living quarters in droves, gathering for exercises outside in the open spaces before they ride off on their bicycles to the work place.

We were told in the hospital or clinics, when we observed the doctors' rounds, that as the patient practiced daily exercise, even if it had to be more of a mental, bed-ridden practice, they were then more open to receiving the healing energy directed from the doctor's hands in treatment.

In a very real sense, I believe that the patients in our own United States hospitals who, on their own, are programmed to relax and live in a state of meditative serenity, are the ones who heal the more readily. Wherever, whether in China or the United States, doctor-patient cooperation in Healing Energy *awareness* is highly significant in renewing physical health. Weigh that against the patient who subconsciously "blames" the doctor for his/her pain. Or, conversely, the doctor who subconsciously "blames" the patient for being too passive in the healing process.

On our second day in Beijing, we visited Guang An Men Hospital where we met with the director of the Academy of Traditional Chinese Medicine, Dr. Qi Li Yi. She had been the mentor of our tour guide, Pamela Murphy, when Pam studied at the Academy for four months a year or two earlier.

Dr. Qi Li Yi was a gracious lady who greeted Pam as a much loved and respected former pupil and colleague. She was very loving and receptive to all of us. For me it was a high moment to present to her my published book, YOUR RADIANT BODY, in its bright yellow cover. She carried it in her hand all the way as she led us on a tour to observe her department.

Patients there included one with an infection of the retina. For her a relatively successful treatment, still in progress, was moxibustion. This method utilized the burning of a processed herb, called moxa. In this case it was used to heat an inserted acupuncture needle. Moxa is used to "disperse cold and damp and tonify blood." We were told that experiments prove it possible to raise the red blood cell count by burning moxa over selective points for several successive days. Red blood cells in circulating throughout the body carry life sustaining oxygen. Moxa is often used for weak or cold patients, and is especially helpful for treating joint problems and arthritis.

Dr. Qi also introduced us to a good-sized herbal pharmacy, an adjunct to the Academy of Traditional Chinese Medicine at Guang An Men Hospital. The herbs were stored in small drawers built into and filling a very large wall. Within the drawers were various herbs used in traditional Chinese prescriptions.

Herbal medicines, called cao yao, in literal translation meaning "medicine from plants," undergird the traditional Chinese healing practice. We are told that there are more than 2,000 substances available in the Chinese pharmaceutical science of herbal medicines. Most are herbs (from plants), but also included are substances from deer antlers, snake gallbladders, shark fins, beetles, cicada, and scorpion, to name a few of the unusual.

Dr. David Eisenberg writes in his ENCOUNTERS WITH QI that the feeling seems to be that Western medicines are fast acting, powerful remedies, but what makes them less desirable is their dangerous side effects. Herbal preparations, by contrast, are "more natural, far less dangerous, slower and gentler in action, but equally or more effective."

Beijing Institute of Technology

Our travel director, Marguerite Craig, had toured the Beijing Institute of Technology with a group in September of 1986 when they met with Professor Xie Huan Zhang. He reported in this meeting in September of 1988 that in the past two years he had received many reports on Qi Gong science in China. Interest and activity was definitely increasing, according to Professor Xie.

A conference of the National Qi Gong Research Institute had just been completed in Sichuan Province, and also conferences had been held in Beijing and Shanghai. Dr. Xie had written a book, SCIENTIFIC BASIS OF QI GONG. At that time it had been published in Chinese in Hong Kong, but not yet translated into English. He explained that chapter nine of his book dealt with the influence of Qi Gong on modern medical science and had the latest information based on his research since 1987.

Professor Xie told us that conventional physical law of healing deals primarily with static, non-living substances and materials. Qi Gong science, in contrast, he explained, is treating life. It works with the vital body energy of Qi. He believes that Qi Gong science will reform present healing science with new laws leading to a scientific revolution, worldwide, in the 21st Century.

We observed a series of Thermovision photos taken of a Qi Gong practitioner's head as he went into a Qi state: Three minutes into this state, a bright spot appeared above his head. At 17 minutes the bright spot was 4 times larger, and at 30 minutes was again 4 times larger; plus a small spot appeared to the right of the large one.

Professor Xie felt this proved that the vital energy of Qi doesn't obey the conventional law of the dissipation of energy which says that energy will not concentrate by itself. In his judgment the pictures showed that entropy can be decreased without loss of energy, and can be concentrated where it is not normally seen. Entropy, he believes, is decreasing when Qi energy is being called into action. He contends that *Qi Gong practice causes negative entropy to appear.* Practice will encourage negative entropy and thereby prolong life. In a very real sense, Qi Gong practice creates order within a body which formerly in negligence allowed disorder. His belief is that at death, entropy is at the maximum. (The law of entropy states that matter tends to wear out and run down with use.)

Syntropy As Negative (Reverse)/Entropy, Relative to Qi Gong

The negative entropy which Professor Xie refers to has been called syntropy by Dr. Albert Szent-Gyorgyi, world renowned biochemist and two-time Nobel Prize winner.

He has written that there is a "drive in living matter to perfect itself." Dr. Szent-Gyorgyi uses the word "drive" in explaining the ability of life to maintain and improve itself.

Life seeks its level in prime *awareness,* searching for the ultimate.

We quote here from YOUR RADIANT BODY, page 154, in the chapter, "Prime Awareness":

> Where the non-living, according to the principle of entropy, tends to wear out, to run down with use, in syntropy (a reverse entropy), the living organism tends to reach higher and higher levels of organization, order and dynamic harmony. (As Dr. Szent-Gyorgyi postulated in a presentation to colleagues at Columbia University many years ago.)

This is the essence of accepting and adapting to Healing Energy, and of the prime *awareness* which activates Healing Energy.

Again quoting from YOUR RADIANT BODY, page 154:

> Like the legendary Phoenix Bird transcending the ashes of its relentless funeral pyre, prime awareness emerges from the continual burning of mind-dross.

And so in Healing Energy — the essence of the drive to perfect itself — the human organism in Infinite Wisdom and Infinite Love rises from the ashes of limiting thoughts and soars to freedom, sensing the Infinite Energy Field which is All of Life. Quoting from YOUR RADIANT BODY:

> Prime awareness is Eternity Past without regret; Eternity Future without fear; it is living now, organized, orderly, and harmonious — the consciousness at one with All of Life. Confucius said, 'What is past one cannot amend; (but) for the future one can always provide.'

So let go of worry and accept wholeness, mentally and physically. Dr. Szent-Gyorgyi's principle of syntropy ties in with and undergirds Qi Gong.

Three Essentials in Practice of Qi Gong

According to Professor Xie, there are three essentials in the effective practice of Qi Gong. The following material is taken from notes of what he shared with us when we visited him at the Beijing Institute of Technology on September 26, 1988:

1) **Quietness** — A vital prerequisite for all types of practice. Eliminate all disturbances and disturbing thoughts. Enter a state of spiritual calmness and mental tranquility; a state of deeply quiet cerebral cortex by a process of mind adjustment. The degree of depth of the quiet state determines the effect of Qi Gong exercise. You may even lose awareness of the body's position or weight and feel yourself in a state of semi-consciousness. The cerebral cortex is in a state of protective inhibition from emotional upset.

2) **Relaxation** — It is vital to let go of all physical and mental tension, completely relax all muscles, viscera, channels and nerves to a state of natural comfort. Hold head erect gently without stress, shoulders relaxed and dropped naturally, upright spine. Shrug shoulders to relax them further, smile instead of having a long face.

3) **Perseverance** — Persist daily, step by step, not being overanxious for success. Don't keep watching anxiously for results.

Where water flows a channel is naturally formed. The more practice, the more progress. Accurate movement is not that important; practice is.

We saw on our tour of China in three major cities, that there were various methods of practicing Qi Gong, according to the presenting masters. Each method had its merit. Some claimed that their particular technique was the only true way. In that regard, I was reminded of religions which claim they have the only way to God. Both in Chinese Qi Gong and in world religions, let us claim autonomy: whatever works for you or me, that is the most acceptable in our individual experience.

I have not embraced any particular Qi Gong method of treatment, but I wholeheartedly believe in the overall principle that it does enhance healing *awareness*. It does so when put to the test in which the individual fully cooperates by practicing the three essentials as stated.

Specific Cures Through Qi Gong

At the time of our tour visit in the fall of 1988, there was no information on treatment of AIDs. It was reported that they did not yet have cases of AIDs in China.

But a great amount of research had been done on cancer. We visited the Sanatoria for Treatment of Cancer and Aged in the country outside of Beijing. This center was begun in 1984 and was not financed by the government. It is yet another research center for the effectiveness of Qi Gong. Here they combine Qi Gong with traditional Chinese medicine in the treatment of cancer, particularly with elderly patients. At the time we were there in 1988 they reported having had some 800 patients and claimed a success rate of healing at 83%. They call "success" the control of cancer or prevention of its getting worse, not cure. Reportedly 39% are getting well — being cured — and the remainder go into remission.

They spoke of the cancer shrinking and in some cases disappearing within a 3-month treatment period. Of those who stayed 6 months or longer, 40% had their symptoms controlled. In this healing category, lung cancer was number 1 and liver cancer was number 2. They also reported the treatment of brain cancer, cancer of the stomach and of the lymph system (which is part of the immune system). Because of the severity of these cases, they were not readily accepted by hospitals, we were told.

Chinese herbal medicine is an important adjunct to the Qi Gong treatment; they also utilize Western medicine wherever it can add to their effectiveness. They cited a number of specific cases.

I had an interesting experience on our visit to this rural Sanatoria: After several leaders had given an hour's presentation about the Sanatoria, we went outside to observe some of the groups engaged in Qi Gong exercise. There were different methods in practice. One was a group of walking Qi Gong patients that particularly appealed to me. They were using a repetition of dance steps resembling a walking-dance pattern. Very rhythmic, which appealed to me. Adapting to their steps, I moved into the rhythm of their method, in an area adjacent to the group action but not within it. I soon found myself being drawn into a kind of trance-like feeling. Within minutes, one of the women doctors at the Sanatoria fell into step beside me, smiling and nodding in greeting. She had powerful Qi energy, and I felt mesmerized by the healing energy as produced by our affinity for each other. It was exhilarating. We continued to walk together for some fifteen minutes or more.

When the group exercise treatment ended, she and I sat together on a garden bench in a beautiful non-verbal exchange. Many of the Chinese exercisers clustered around us. It was non-verbal between us because she could not speak my language, nor I hers. Yet our mutual exchange of Healing Energy drew us together.

With my white hair and elderly appearance, one elderly Chinese patient was prompted to step close to us and with a Chinese doctor as interpreter, told me it was his 70th birthday. I told him that was exactly my age, and that opened a flood-gate of mutual admiration and explanation by him on how he had been healed of cancer there at the Sanatoria.

For the brief moments of that delightful and stimulating encounter, I was one with the Chinese people — seemingly one with All of Life. The lady doctor, who had walked with me in the treatment exercise, smiled and nodded while the English interpretation continued. When it was time to board the bus, she and

I embraced as if we had been friends for a very long time — perhaps we had been in a former lifetime. Her spirit energies were with me all the way back to the reality of Beijing.

The Life Energy of Qi As Life Information

Professor Xie of the Beijing Institute of Technology believes that Qi is Life Information, as he calls it. For example, he has applied his Qi Gong research to agriculture. He showed us photos of rice seeds treated with Qi Gong energy which indicated that even those grown in drought areas grew better than untreated seeds. In this treatment experiment, seeds are treated with Qi energy in a complicated process before they are planted. Control groups of untreated seeds are planted in the same area. He reported that Qi energy increased the production of sugar beets 43% and of soybeans, 54%. When they used a control person who doesn't practice Qi Gong, simulating the treatment process on the seeds, there was no effect.

Professor Xie also showed us photos of cucumber plants that had been treated with the Life Information of Qi. They sprouted three original leaves instead of the normal two. He said that throughout the plant world seeds normally sprout with only one or two original leaves except when treated with Qi energy.

In his presentation at the Beijing Institute of Technology, Professor Xie told us that the three organizers of everything in the universe are 1) energy, 2) material, and 3) information. For the past many years, he said to us, only material and energy have been considered by humanity.

In the 20th Century, the emphasis has been on an information flow which is very significant in investigating life energy. I interpret this information flow as pertinent to what we speak of as enhancing *awareness* in order to more fully activate the Healing Energy.

Professor Xie is experimenting to see if Qi produced by emanation is mainly information instead of energy. He believes the practitioner is transmitting cellular information to the patient's cells rather than energy per se. He said if energy were doing the healing, then since an infrared lamp transmits much more energy than the practitioner's hand, the lamp should heal, and it doesn't.

He measures information flow with an experiment on variations of modulation of energy, claiming a dynamic change means increased information flow. He said the health of the practitioner also alters the ability of Qi to send information.

As I hear it coming through from Infinite Wisdom, a significant change in the greater Energy Field of the macrocosm is awakening a stored energy-memory of the DNA within the individual human cell. This will activate a greater healing potential for humanity. This will only be effective for those who believe in and *trust* in greater *awareness* through Infinite Wisdom.

As we observed the Qi Gong masters and listened to the research results of what that master could achieve in emanating Life Energy, I was reminded that each of us has a continuing responsibility to heal self so that we may become healers of the world.

There seems to be no end to the benefits of Qi Gong, even as in holism when we practice it in Radiant Living and in other similar disciplines in the United States.

Another example of where the Chinese have applied Qi energy is with retardates to increase their learning ability. We are using similar measures in the United States. We are also using meditative awareness in our country to enhance the students' ability to relax and recall studied material in writing exam questions. I have personally used that holistic component both in pre-exam study and exam writing. In pre-exam study, I was suddenly *aware* of a phase of the subject that would be included in the exam. In writing the exam, later, it was amazing to me when that would prove to be valid. One particular instance I recall was in my statistics course which was extremely difficult for me. One question that nearly everyone missed was entirely clear to me because of the pre-exam study awareness. It never would have been otherwise, for it was a phase of the subject I'd never paid much attention to.

Pertinent Facts on Acupuncture As Healing and Adaptive Measures

Acupuncture is a significant part of the 5,000 year old Chinese medical system. The traditional use of it was to prevent illness and to enhance health.

In prevention, acupuncture is subtle enough to detect mild physiological imbalances of major organs very often long before any serious symptoms are present. Thus treatment may be applied to strengthen any weakness and to harmonize the imbalance. There are thirteen body systems and when they are all in synchrony, the harmony of health prevails. Acupuncture is a means of detecting the absence of synchrony in these body systems.

Acupuncture in the United States is becoming a practical healing method through its use by more than five thousand certified practitioners nationwide. Several insurance companies reportedly now reimburse patients for their treatment expense. This speaks to the acceptance in our country.

My notes from information gleaned on my Chinese tour indicate that traditional Chinese acupuncturists use nine different kinds of needles at different body sites for various therapeutic purposes.

These very fine stainless steel needles are mostly one to two inches long, although some may be as long as four to five inches. For a treatment, usually two to four needles are put at different points and twirled alternately. The example given was of a treatment for heart disease: one needle might be used specifically to stabilize the heartbeat, one to lower blood pressure, and one to tranquilize the mind.

The acupuncturist is trained to know the correct point of bodily contact for any given ailment. They must select from some 365 acupoints which connect along any of the 14 major meridians as lines of energy flow. There are another 57 secondary meridians in a complete network.

The only pain experienced in acupuncture is when the needle goes through the skin. Once the needle(s) are inserted the patient is alert to a feeling of fullness, tingling, or numbness. Such feelings indicate that the needle is in the right place. The acupuncturist waits for the patient to indicate this.

Acupuncture may well be one of the oldest medical treatments.

In use some 3,000 years, it was reportedly practiced even before the great pyramids were built. In the last 25 years, acupuncture has been used as an effective surgical analgesic.

As an example of this, acupuncture was cited as the sole analgesic in a case of surgery in removing a lung. Four acupuncturists twirled 40 needles to keep the patient anesthetized. It was completely effective, even though no one could explain why.

As for the theory of acupuncture's validity as a general stabilizer, the Chinese claim that health depends on the flow of Qi, meaning the life-energy, along invisible pathways called jing — or meridians. When this flow is disrupted, pain and/or disease is the result. A disrupted energy flow may manifest in chronic tension syndromes such as a headache, tight muscles, improper bowel function, etc. Scientifically, acupuncture relates to the body physiology by inducing hormonal reflex mechanisms and by blocking nerve impulses. This induces increasing uniform blood flow and a decrease in muscular tension.

On average, an acupuncture treatment may last from 20 to 40 minutes with the patient stretched out on a treatment table. Once the needles are inserted, they may be simply left in place, or may be stimulated and removed after a few moments, or in a matter of longer time.

There are several methods of stimulation: 1) manual manipulation by turning, 2) electrical impulse, or 3) by a thermal method, as already explained, called moxibustion. Both the manual turning and the electrical impulse are designed to "move the energy" and to relieve congestion. Moxibustion basically applies heat to the area being treated.

Important to the success of the treatment, the patient should, on treatment day, avoid coffee, alcohol, and stimulants of all kinds. Hot baths or strenuous exercise should be avoided just before the treatment.

Acupuncture tends to have a cumulative effect, so treatments are normally given in a series. Six to twelve are a usual course. For best results, the treatments begin with two weekly for the first three weeks. Following that routine they are scheduled once a week, and then progressively at greater intervals. The entire course of treatment may last several weeks, several months, or in response to a chronic condition, as long as a year.

Recovery time depends upon the length of the illness, severity, and the age of the patient. Occasionally as a part of the healing process, a patient may experience temporary aggravation of their symptoms, but that is usually followed by rapid improvement.

The major aim of the treatment is to relieve not only the symptoms but to correct the root cause, as well, helping the body to return to a harmonious state of health which will perpetuate itself, long term.

In an acupuncture treatment there are two important things to do: 1) relax, and 2) observe. *Relax* and breathe deeply and fully with your abdomen. *Observe* any changes in your body, any new sensations. Stay relaxed without trying to change these sensations. Simply observe and allow it to happen.

Imagination. It is also very helpful to imagine those sensations changing the energy circulation in your body, so that the energy is circulating more freely. Your imagination is as important as the acupuncture needles in stimulating natural healing.

In Summary

Even as you and I marvel at the inherited body physiology which so adequately heals and/or sustains our physical disability, others blatantly scoff at its reality.

The belief system is crucial. For those who scoff, there is no validity to this whole chapter. Denial is a bummer. It is equivalent to saying there is no sun when the dark of night enshrouds the earth.

I write this bleak note because I hear the evidence all around me. Such bleakness is frequently encouraged by features in the popular press. A recent newspaper article spoke this very message in regard to Qi Gong. It appeared in the "Worldview" section of the local newspaper. The gentleman who wrote it had visited China and talked to a master of Qi Gong. He wrote about visiting the rooms where the master worked with his patients. The writer called the master a doctor. His description of his work was a "tongue in cheek" approach. He did not say the man is weird, he merely writes it so that the reader can hardly see him as anything more than that, especially if it is his/her introduction to Qi Gong:

To enter (the doctor's rooms) is to cross a very strange threshold indeed. (The writer goes on to strip him of professional dignity): There is Li, standing in a corner, sucking in his breath and jabbing with his arms like a conjurer, a fierce expression of concentration on his face.

And there is his patient of the moment...partly paralyzed by a stroke, swaying, dancing, flapping his arms like a marionette being yanked by invisible strings. His Adam's apple bobs up and down and his eyes are shut tight.

Healing and adapting to pain are in the eyes of the beholder as well as in the mind of the believer. The one who sees it all as fraud, as another of life's silly white lies, cannot benefit from his/her own inheritance. Our healing power inheritance does not function unless it is activated by a believing mental process. It is entirely up to the individual to believe or disbelieve according to the *awareness* of the moment.

Where I am particularly saddened is that some will read that article and store away the "weird" aspect of Qi Gong. Without further knowledge to the contrary they cannot do otherwise.

So the summary statement is to entreat all to sift carefully the new concepts that evolve in this transitional decade of new information, the years of the 1990s.

If you are young enough now to be living at least half of your lifetime in the 21st Century, you are going to be confronted with many "weird" practices. There may be those who wrongfully desecrate some of it, but in responsible hands, these unfamiliar approaches will be helping humanity to evolve into a vast new *awareness* of their healing potential. And alas for the man-made laws which try to negate their power.

There is so much in this world that needs healing. It cannot be made whole by using antiquated tools. Let's you and I give healing a chance — personally and worldwide — by planting seeds of wisdom in the minds of those who scoff. Best of all, we can be role models.

The more I study Qi Gong, Acupuncture, and Moxibustion, the more I believe in the validity of the Chinese healing arts. They are as simple and yet as profound as the Holistic approach of Radiant

Living and the other similar disciplines practiced in the United States. Let us weave them together along with all the other significant practices so that we may heal the world, or at the very least help everyone to *adapt* to disease or disability that will not let go — in this lifetime.

EPILOGUE

Anticipating The Global Family

Radiant Living anticipates that in the 21st Century, countries of the world will bond together as a Global Family.
Competition for power will fade into cooperation for Peace. Human dignity will be restored.
This does not suppose that perfect harmony will obliterate all disagreement, but, rather, that mediation will become a learned and acceptable artform. Peaceful coexistence will triumph.

The pattern for all of this will emerge from individual family units as we presently know them. No one of these smaller units has perfect unity, but Wisdom and Love can *change* hostility into tranquility. They can with responsible discipline that puts such components into practice. In the 21st Century, known alternately as the Age of Aquarius or the Age of Enlightenment, the pattern for bonding in individual family units will blossom into a viable pattern for the Global Family.

In Radiant Living, Infinite Wisdom and Infinite Love have been relentlessly put to the test for change. I know from my own experience that they work. I also know from the feedback of countless others.

Spirit entities are even now guiding this work of global bonding through human energy. Our civilization will survive because more and more caring people commit their full potential to it. These people work wherever they are, in whatever arena they have chosen for this life's achievement.

The geneology of the Global Family will portray a wide divergence, a fact that definitely contributes to its Power. Shared talents of all ethnic groups will meld for Good.

When this natural, universal lifestyle is established, the starving will be nourished from food of their own creation; the homeless will be housed as they labor for their ultimate need, and the worldwide discontent of the 20th Century will be eased in accordance with human dignity. Everyone will have a chance.

Dynamic energy is even now heralding this phenomenal change, and all who "listen" can hear it. Once they do, there's no turning back. The energy is electric and the current continues to intensify. The issue of bonding is being understood in a new and creative way.

I witnessed it personally during my travels within the Soviet Union in 1987, and in my subsequent visit to the People's Republic of China in 1988. Our English language lacks words to describe the depth of feelings that continues as a flame within me.

I came home to see Radiant Living in a new Burst of Light.

This book was in process long before my journeys, and while I was abroad I attempted again and again to put into my notes the change I felt at the very core of my being. I could not express it.

Further, in my writing during the months after I returned, I could not keep abreast of the rapid and meaningful global changes. Finally, I am content to end with this epilogue. There is no use to say how it is today because by tomorrow today will be obsolete. This is the decade of *change,* rapid and decisive.

Radiant Living is a catalyst for change. It is, indeed, embodied in and empowered by that change. I feel fulfilled within its flow of Infinite Wisdom and Infinite Love as they have become dominant in my life.

As you come home to Radiant Living, may you find similar joy in your own interpretation, and in the freedom you find to be in charge of your life.